MODULAR SCI[ENCE] fo[r GCSE]

MODULE Electricity in action

Many devices have been designed to exploit the properties of electricity. The picture above shows a close-up of the filament of a light bulb. When electricity flows through the filament it gets white hot, giving out a bright white light. This module looks at many properties of electricity and how to make good use of them.

Spread

Relevant National Curriculum Attainment Target: AT4

1 Why electricity?

Electricity is just one of the many forms of energy. Why do we use so much of it? Not because it's cheap.

We buy coal by the tonne, gas by the therm, oil by the gallon, and electricity by the **kilowatt hour**. This means it's not easy to compare these energy sources to see which is the cheapest. But if you work out the energy in each as the number of **megajoules** (MJ) which you get for each pound of money, you can see that electricity is in a class of its own – as by far the dearest!

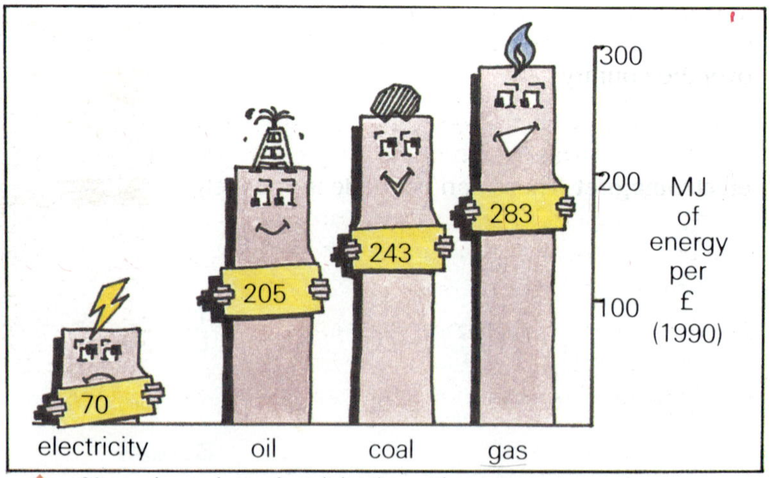

£1 produces less electricity than other energy sources.

At the flick of a switch . . .

Despite the cost, we use so much electricity because it's just so convenient. It is easy to convert it into any other form of energy we might need.

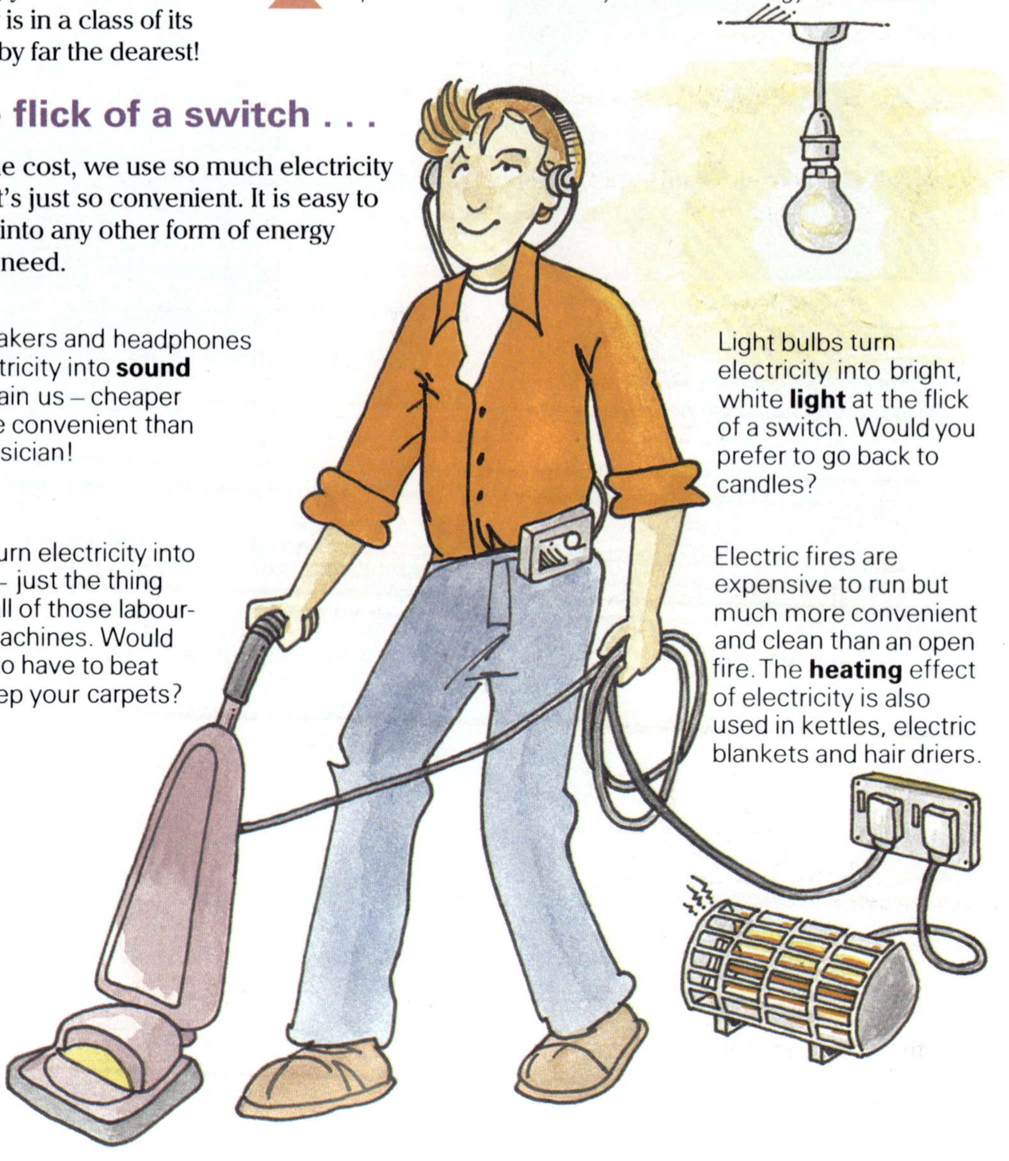

Loudspeakers and headphones turn electricity into **sound** to entertain us – cheaper and more convenient than a live musician!

Motors turn electricity into **motion** – just the thing to drive all of those labour-saving machines. Would you like to have to beat and sweep your carpets?

Light bulbs turn electricity into bright, white **light** at the flick of a switch. Would you prefer to go back to candles?

Electric fires are expensive to run but much more convenient and clean than an open fire. The **heating** effect of electricity is also used in kettles, electric blankets and hair driers.

At home and at work

Electricity powers the transmitters that beam TV and radio programmes into our homes. The transmitters turn electrical energy into **electromagnetic waves** which spread out all over the country.

Wind a coil of wire around some iron, switch on the electricity – and you have an simple **electromagnet**. These can be made immensely strong, enough to lift heavy scrap iron. They can also be used to create the pictures on your TV, or even as part of a brain scanner.

Electrical energy is also used to extract reactive metals from their ores. Without electricity there would be no aluminium for saucepans or planes.

Powerful electromagnets move heavy scrap iron.

Don't forget electronics!

Computers, stereos, videos, compact disc players, digital watches, synthesisers, radio alarm clocks, automatic washing machines, video games . . .

Electricity is pretty useful stuff – this module will help you to find out more about it.

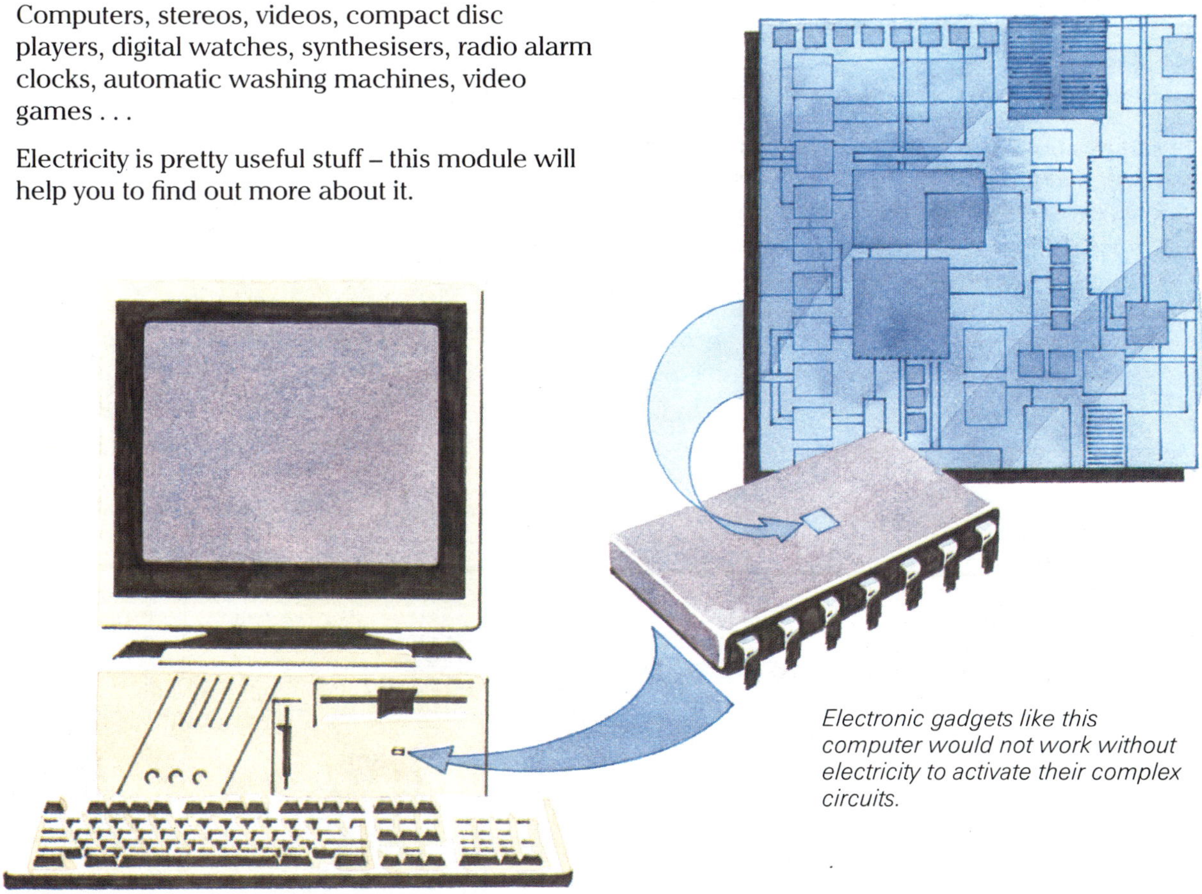

Electronic gadgets like this computer would not work without electricity to activate their complex circuits.

1 Think of the five things you use most each day that use electricity. How would you cope in each case if there was no electricity?

2 Count up the number of electrical devices you have at home (count both battery- and mains-powered devices). Which room has the most? Which one has the least? Suggest why these rooms have so many or so few.

2 So what is electricity?

You can't touch, taste, see, smell or hear electricity directly – but you can often see what it does. What could be going on to cause all these different effects?

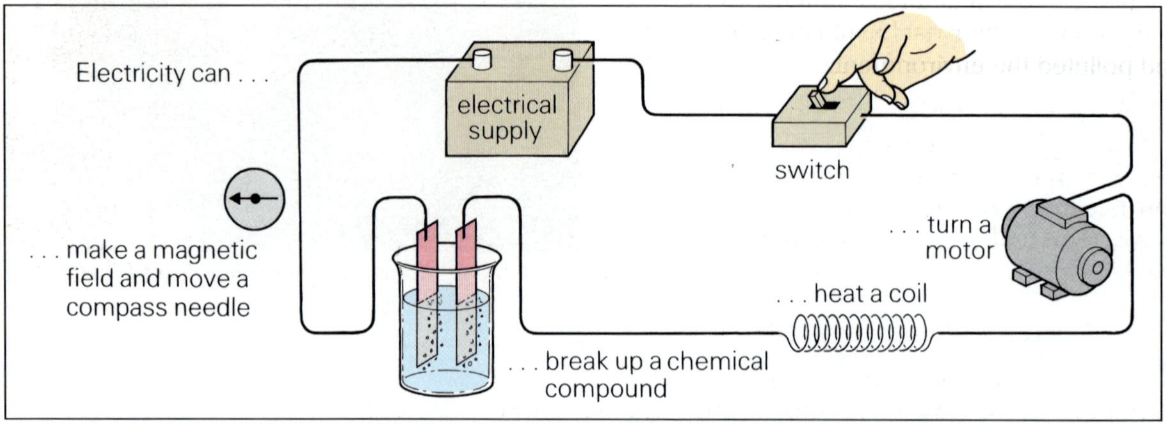

Static and spark

To get an idea about what might be happening, let's think about a different kind of electricity. Have you ever had a small electric shock as you've reached for a door-handle after walking over a nylon carpet? Or heard a crackling sound and seen flashes of light as you've pulled off a nylon jumper? (And you certainly will have seen lightning, which is just a bigger version of the same thing!) You've probably been told: 'That's static electricity!' But what does that mean?

Electrical charges

All substances contain electrical **charges**. These come in two opposite kinds – we call them **positive** (+) and **negative** (–). These charges are normally present in equal numbers and so cancel each other out. But if you rub two different materials together – such as shoe leather and nylon – it is possible to knock some charges from one to the other and so upset this balance.

All these opposite charges attract each other – they try to get back together. If enough of them have collected, they will have enough energy to 'jump' a small gap as a spark.

Static can be useful . . .

Have you ever noticed how dusty TV screens get? The dust is attracted to them by the static charge that builds up there.

This static attraction is put to good use in coal-fired power stations, which use it in their chimneys to trap dirt and dust particles. Here electrostatic precipitators trap tonnes of material every day that otherwise would have poured out and polluted the environment.

Another good use is in photocopying machines. Light falling onto a special material gives a negative image in static charge! This is then transferred to a drum and powdered ink is made to stick to it, which is then rolled onto paper.

This fine powder forms an image by static.

. . . or very dangerous

Static charges can form wherever different materials move against one another – even where liquids flow through pipes. And where charges build up, sparking can occur.

When aircraft are refuelled, thousands of gallons of aviation fuel are pumped at high speed through fuelpipes. Any charge building up here could spark to the metal of the aircraft with catastrophic results. To stop this happening, the pumps, pipes and aircraft are first linked together by a metal cable, which is then '**earthed**' (as will be explained later). Any charge formed now can be led away safely through the metal, and so dangerous sparking will not occur.

. . . even for computers

The large static charges in lightning can play havoc with electronic equipment. Burglar alarms may be set off, computers may 'crash' and the microchips within them may be damaged permanently.

On a smaller scale, microelectronic devices must always be protected from electrostatic sparking. It has been known for office computers to blow up because of the disruption caused by static produced from their operator's nylon underwear!

Static charges could build up in aircraft fuelpipes, but the earth lead clamped to the front wheel prevents any build up.

1 What are the different effects that can be caused by an electric current?

2 How can we charge things up with static electricity? Explain what is happening.

3 What good uses can be made of electrostatic attraction?

4 Why do static charges sometimes lead to sparking? Why can this be dangerous?

5 How can electrostatic charges be discharged safely?

3 What else is involved?

Conductors and insulators

Static charges build up on some materials, such as plastics or rubber, because any charges 'knocked' onto them get stuck on the surface and are not free to move. We call these materials **insulators**.

Other materials, such as metals or carbon, however, allow the much smaller negative charges to move around within them. We call these materials **conductors**.

It is when negative charges move through a conductor that we say a **current** of electricity is flowing. We call these small, negative charges **electrons**.

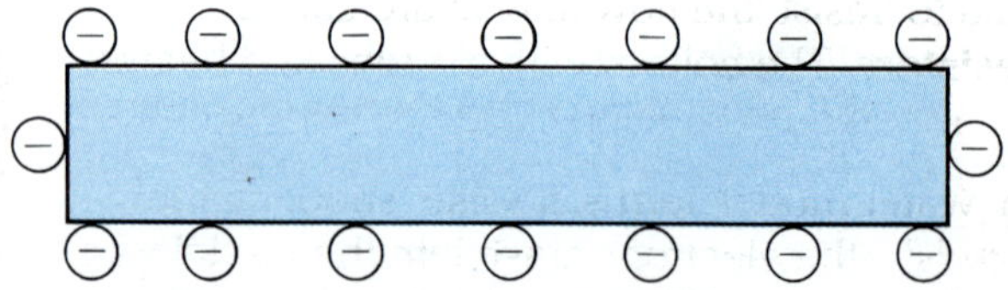

charges on an insulator

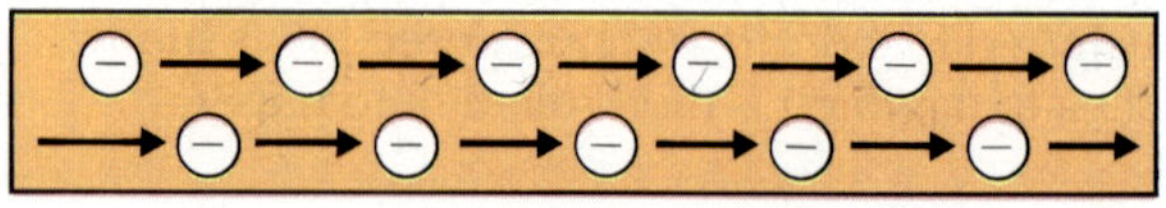

charges moving within a conductor (not to scale)

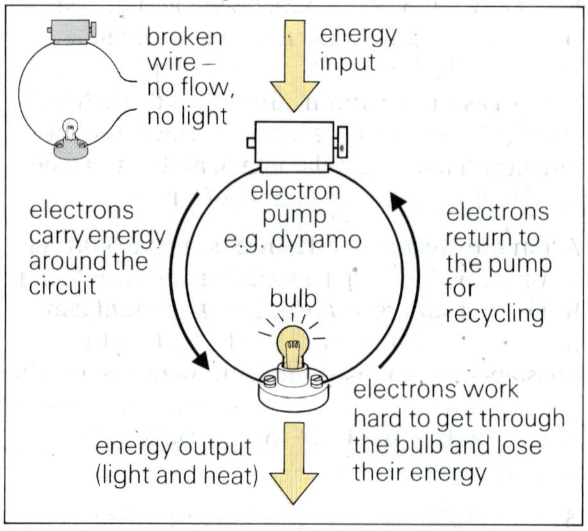

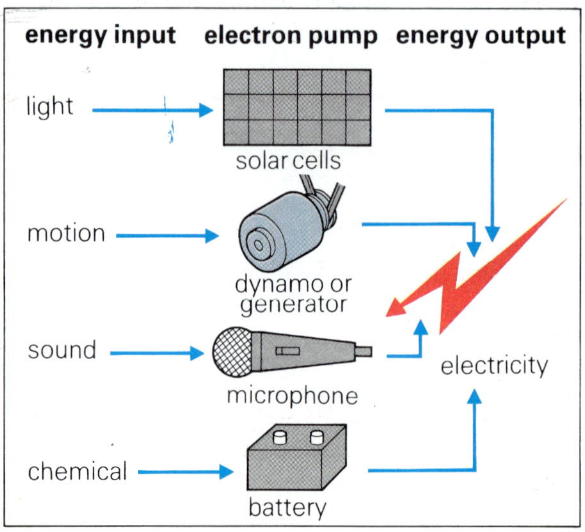

Pumping charge – current electricity

The flow of electrons through a metal wire is often likened to the flow of water along a pipe. A hose full of water does not become 'useful' until the water is made to move. To make the water move, you need a pump, and that means energy is needed to work the pump.

Similarly, a disconnected wire is full of electrons, but some kind of 'pump' is needed to make an electric current flow, and an energy source is needed to drive it. You probably use many things powered by **batteries**. These use chemical reactions to produce the energy to pump the charges through your radio, Walkman and so on.

Recycling electrons

To use current electricity, there has to be a continuous connection from one terminal of the 'electron pump', through conducting wires to whatever is being worked by the electricity – a bulb, for example – and back through wires to the other terminal of the 'pump'. This is called a **circuit** and, as the name suggests, electrons flow around it. Break it at any point, and the flow stops – that's how **switches** work.

In this way, electrons are recycled – used over and over again – and are given a new 'kick' of energy each time they pass through the 'pump'. It is this energy which is given up to the bulb and turned into heat and light.

Why do heating coils and bulbs get hot?

Many materials conduct electricity to some extent, but do not allow it to pass freely. They are said to 'resist' the flow and so are called **resistors**. The coils of wire in bulbs and heaters are made from special resistance wire like this.

In 'water model' terms, it's like 'shooting the rapids' – the electrons crash into the particles in the wire, giving up some of their energy as heat before moving on. This makes the wire heat up. The wires in light bulbs are designed to get so hot that they get 'white hot', and give off white light!

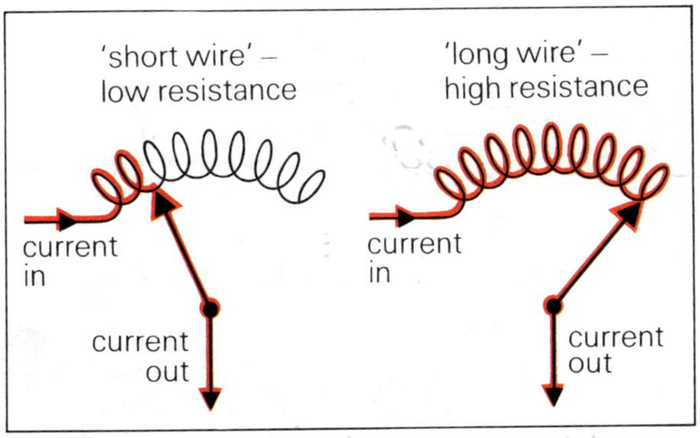

Resistance and control

If a second bulb is added to a simple circuit, both bulbs now glow more dimly than before. This is because the extra bulb *increases* the overall resistance in the circuit, so the 'pump' is unable to push as much current around, and less heat is generated. Any extra resistance added into the circuit will have a similar effect, and this can be used to control the brightness of lamps.

A 'dimmer switch' works by passing the current driving a bulb through a **variable resistor**. When turned to a *low* resistance, a *large* current can flow and the bulb glows brightly. But, as the resistance is increased, the current drops and the bulb becomes dimmer. The volume control on a radio and the speed control of a model railway work in a similar way.

Some variable resistors have a long coil of resistance wire inside them. A sliding contact can vary the length of wire that the current must pass along, and so vary the resistance.

Inside a 'dimmer' switch.

1 What are the differences between conductors and insulators?

2 Why is it only the negative charges that move through a conductor?

3 What is an 'electron pump'? Give some examples.

4 How do resistors differ from simple conductors and insulators?

5 What happens to the flow of current in a circuit:
- **a** if the circuit breaks
- **b** if extra resistance is added?

6 Why does a heating element get hot when current flows?

4 Circuit shorthand

A tip from the tube

If you wanted to find out how to get from New Cross to Leicester Square on the London Underground, you could look at an accurate street map and try to follow the lines and stations as they snake around and cross. Or you could just look at the Underground map – even though this is not actually accurate in terms of station and line positions and distances! But it does show very clearly which stations are on the same line, and where you can change trains – which is all that you actually need to know. It also uses standard symbols for stations, British Rail links, time restrictions, and so on, which make it easier to find the information you need.

London regional Transport User Number 92/1586

Electricians face a similar problem. The wires connecting pieces of electrical apparatus can get very messy – 'benchtop spaghetti' is a common description! Even if you could draw this accurately, would it be clear from the drawing what was going on? No!

So electricians, too, resort to an agreed, *stylised* way of representing the information that really counts – showing which parts are electrically connected to which. They also use standard symbols to represent pieces of equipment.

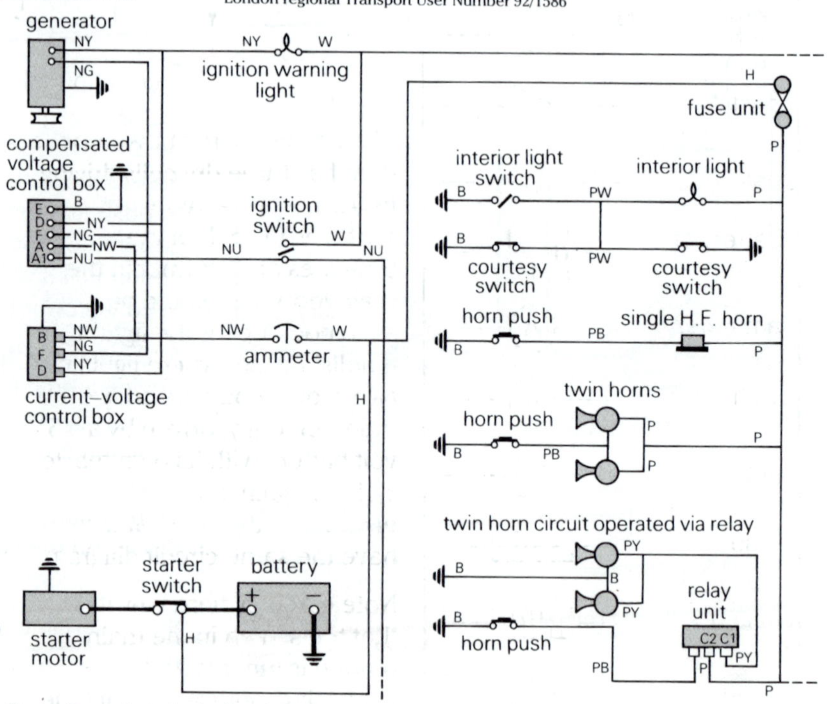

Part of an electrical circuit for a car.

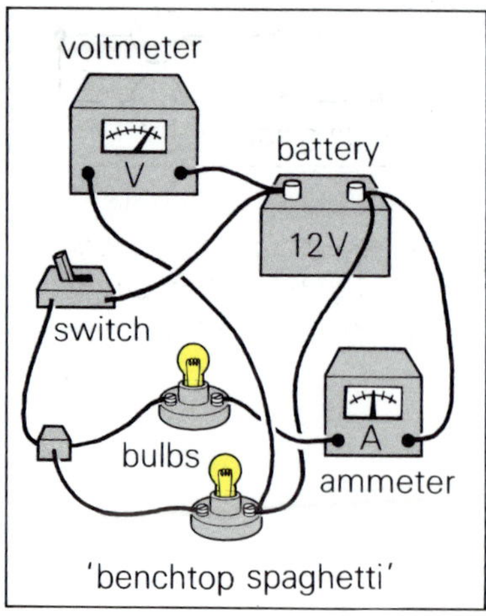

'benchtop spaghetti'

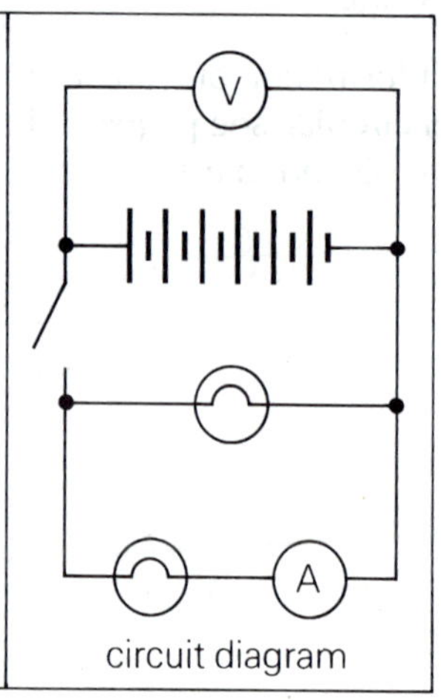

circuit diagram

'Spaghetti' versus style

The **circuit diagrams** produced in this standard style are much easier to follow than more realistic versions – once you get used to using them! The trick is to practise. Try drawing circuit diagrams from 'benchtop spaghetti' and setting up circuits from circuit diagrams as often as possible, then you will soon be totally familiar with them.

Lighting up

It is possible to set up a simple **series** circuit with two dry cells, a bulb, a switch and some connecting wire. This may look very different but, electrically, it is exactly the same as a standard torch circuit, so they have the same circuit diagram. (See right.)

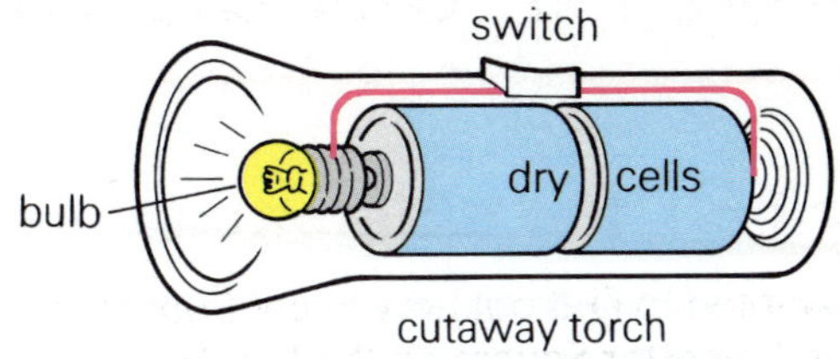

The standard system set.

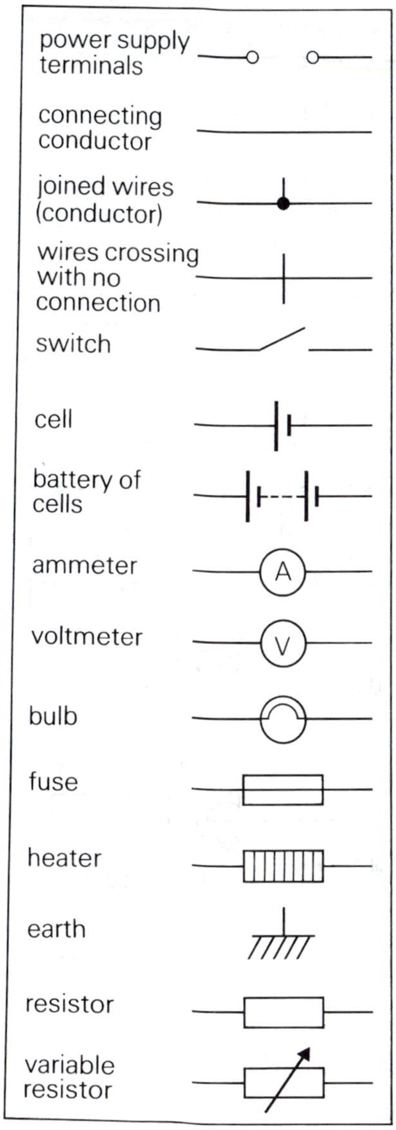

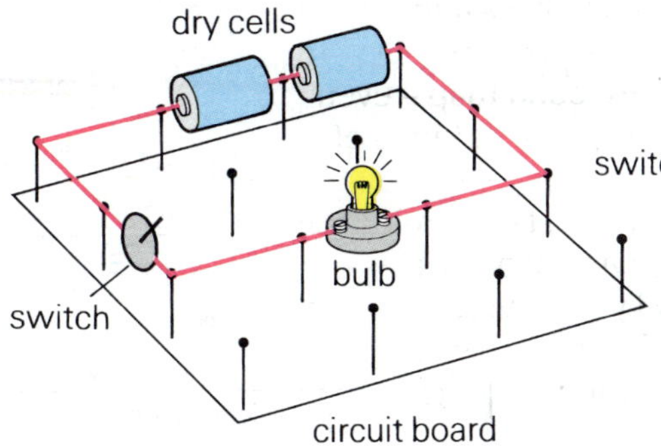

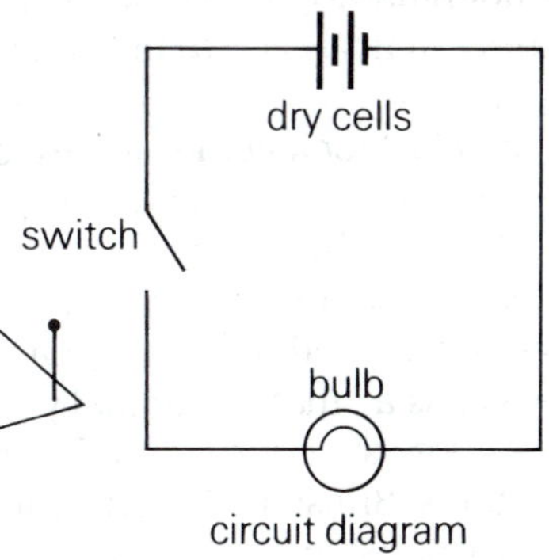

The circuit board shown on the right has three dry cells driving two bulbs in **parallel**, with switches in each of the branches and another in the main loop. This could be used as a mock-up for the lighting in a dolls' house, where lights in two rooms could be controlled independently, driven by a 4.5 volt battery with its own master switch. Again, they are electrically the same and so have the same circuit diagram.

Note carefully here why it is that the switch in the main branch is the 'master' controlling both lamps, but the other switches control the individual lamps.

(For more information on series and parallel circuits, see pages 24–5 later in this module.)

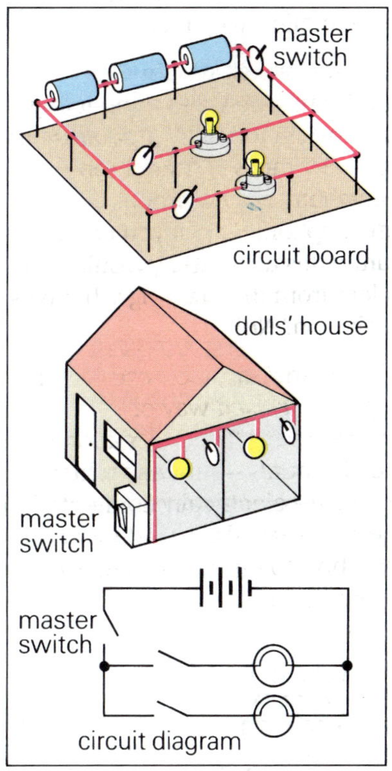

1 Describe how you could get from New Cross to Leicester Square on the London Underground.

2 Draw circuit diagrams for:

a a dry cell, two bulbs, a switch and an ammeter in a series;

b a dynamo working three lamps in parallel.

3 Design a circuit diagram that could work a model set of traffic lights, with separate switches for red, amber and green.

5 Mains electricity

a.c./d.c. – the difference is easy

So far we have talked about current flowing around a circuit. In the case of **batteries**, this is exactly what happens. Electrons leave the *negative* terminal and flow round to the *positive*. This simple flow of charge is called the **direct current** (d.c.).

However, with '**mains**' electricity the electrons move *backwards and forwards* around the circuit. This happens because the driving **voltage** (see page 24) goes through 50 cycles of change every second. This is called an **alternating current** (a.c.). It may seem odd, but for most household uses, it does not matter which way the electrons are moving. As long as they *are* moving, they have enough energy for heating, lighting and driving motors.

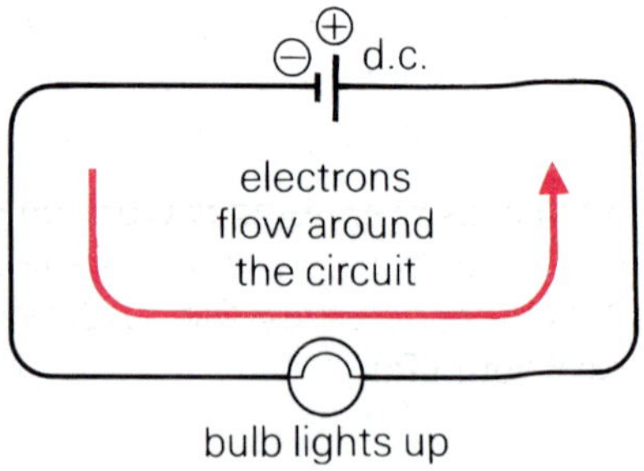

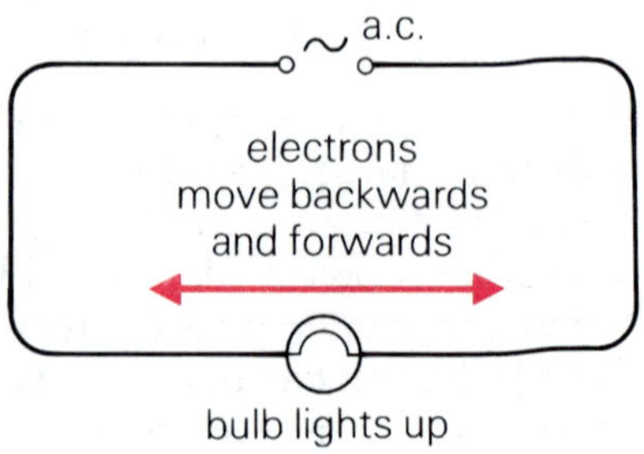

Looking at a.c.

A **cathode ray oscilloscope** (CRO) can show what is happening to the electricity in the wires carrying an alternating current. The CRO turns the a.c. signal into lines on a screen. The voltage in one wire rises and falls – this wire is called the **live wire**. The voltage in the other wire appears to remain constant – so this wire is called the **neutral wire**.

a.c. on a cathode ray oscilloscope.

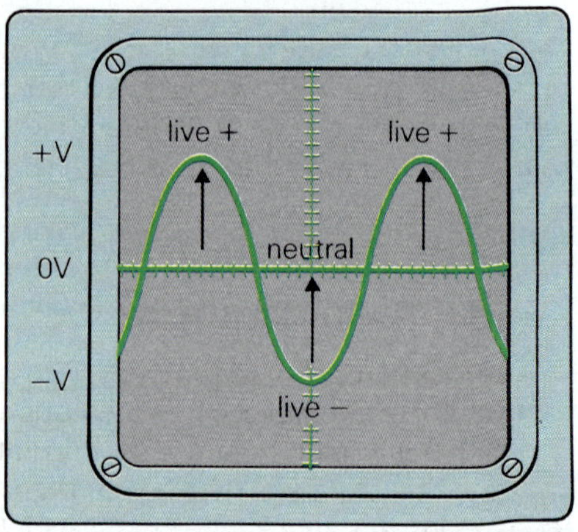

This changing cycle has a similar effect to switching the terminals on a battery – current is driven first one way then the other (from neutral to live, then live to neutral).

The three wires

Mains electricity needs two wires to work, but three wires to be safe. These wires are:

- *Live wire* – this carries the alternating voltage that will drive the current (once connected).
- *Neutral wire* – this is the 'base line': current flows backwards and forwards between this wire and the live wire.
- *Earth wire* – this is the safety wire which helps to protect you from dangerous 'short-circuits'.

It is a matter of life and death that these wires are connected up the right way, so in household equipment they are colour-coded to make this easier to do.

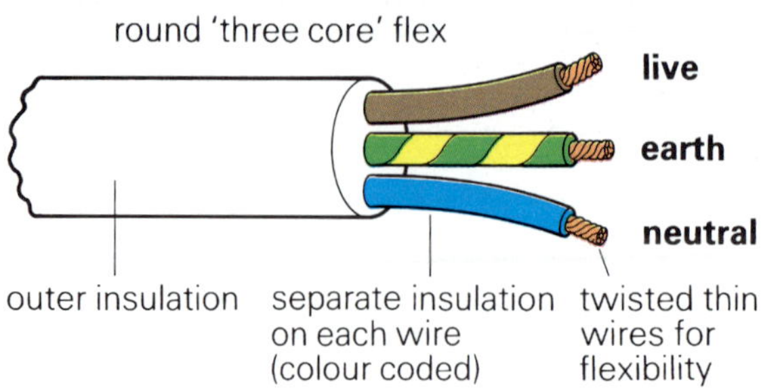

A correctly wired plug.

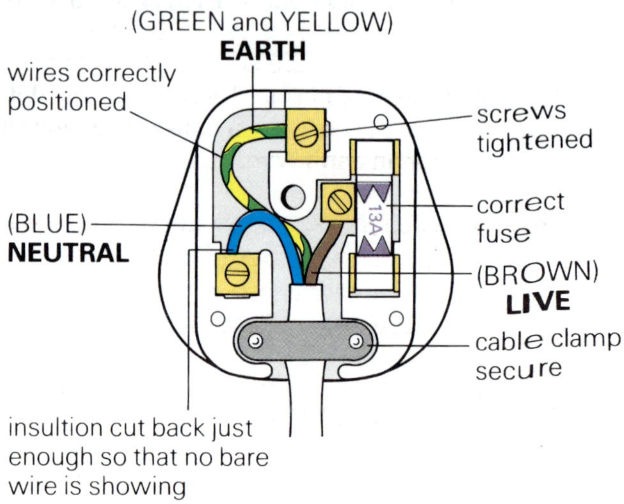

Safety first

If the live wire carries the signal, which returns through the neutral wire – why bother with any others? A kettle connected to just live and neutral would work, so what use is the earth wire?

So long as everything *is* working perfectly, the earth wire has no use. But if a fault occurs in the other two wires, the earth wire could save your life!

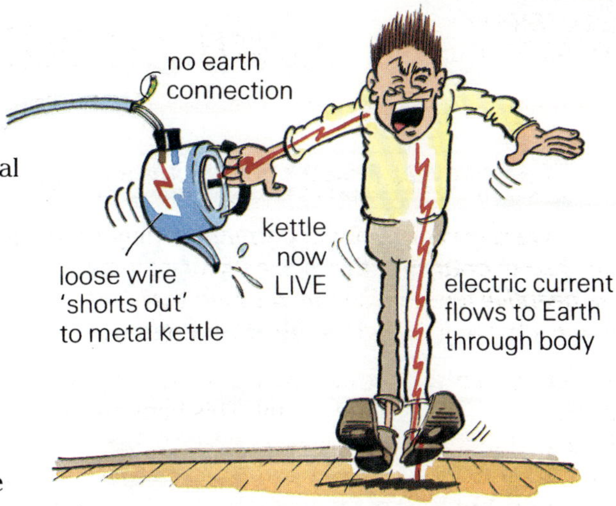

An unconnected earth wire can lead to a nasty shock . . .

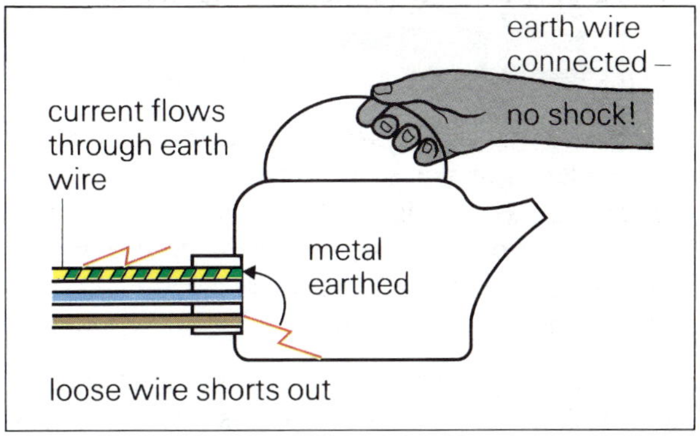

What's the danger?

The current flowing back and forth from the live wire has a 'target' – its target is anything at zero volts. Your body is a conductor, and you are normally in contact with something that is at zero volts – the floor or ground (literally the planet Earth). This contact makes you a target for any stray current from a live wire.

Think about an old metal kettle with just live and neutral wires – say a loose live wire touches the metal of the kettle. This makes the metal of the kettle 'live'. As soon as you touch the metal of this kettle, your body completes a circuit between the live wire and the 'zero volt' planet Earth. All the current flows through you, giving you an **electric shock**.

. . . but not all equipment needs an earth wire

What can be done?

Your body, your shoes, the carpet – none of these are as good a conductor as a copper wire. The copper in the earth wire provides a much better path for any stray current escaping from the live wire. If all metal parts which you might touch are connected to an earth wire, any shock will short-circuit to Earth through the earth wire instead of through you.

Some modern equipment with metal surfaces does not have an earth wire – but it is safe to use. Why? This is because all the parts which use the current are completely sealed off from the outside by a double layer of plastic. This **double insulation** means that there is no risk of shock even if there is a faulty live wire. So there is no need for an earth wire.

1 **a** What are the names of the three wires used in mains electricity?
b How are they colour-coded for household appliances?

2 Decribe how an earth wire could save your life if a fault occurred.

3 Describe the movement of an electron around:
a an a.c. circuit
b a d.c. circuit.

6 Safe as houses?

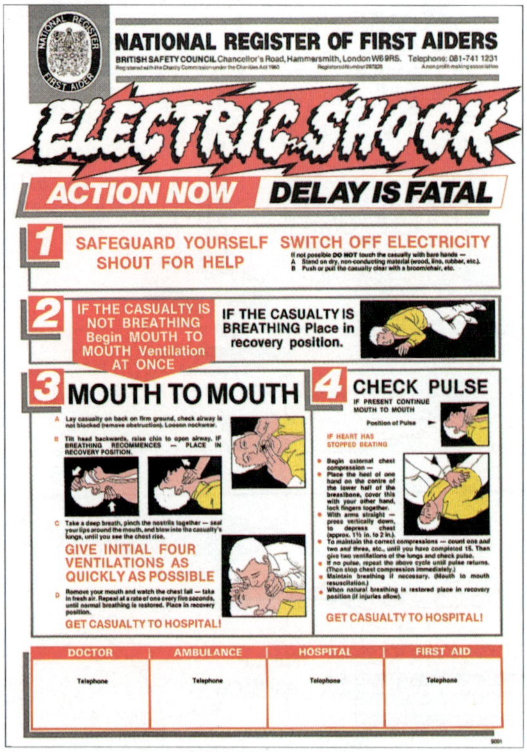

How to treat electric shock.

Just how electrically safe is your home?

We use electricity so much that we often take it for granted and forget just how dangerous it can be.

Consider this incident: 'As the kettle started to boil, Peter reached across from the sink and pulled at the plug. The next thing he knew, he was lying on the floor on the other side of the kitchen!'

Do you know anyone who has had an electric shock? If they were able to tell you about it, they were lucky!

What shocks do

Electric shocks make your muscles contract. This can sometimes clamp your grip on the live equipment, but normally 'throws' you away. Shocks also affect the heart – either stopping it completely or causing it to beat irregularly. Even this can lead to brain damage within 2 to 4 minutes if no action is taken.

What to do

In case of electric shock *switch off the mains supply* and then apply emergency first aid if you know how. Get someone to phone for an ambulance.

(For short courses in emergency first aid, apply to your local branch of the St John Ambulance Brigade.)

Killer in the kitchen

Peter should have switched off the socket, not pulled the plug, but his main problem was wet hands!

Safety regulations state that power sockets should not be fitted in bathrooms or too close to sinks in kitchens. Why is that?

Your body has a fairly low resistance because of all the water it contains. Your only protection is if there is high resistance between your skin and the source of the current, or between you and the ground. Dry hands have a high resistance (and some shoes have a very high resistance) so 'dry' shocks are generally mild. But if your hands are wet a much better electrical contact is made, the resistance is lowered and more current flows – so the shock can be dangerous. And if your feet are wet too you are in danger of getting a fatal shock.

Be a safety sleuth!

Some common causes of electrical accidents are obvious enough – if you know what you are looking for! Watch out for . . .

1. Sockets too close to sinks.
2. Electrical flexes that have become split or frayed. This can happen in time to the wires of vacuum cleaners, irons, kettles, or anything else that is moved around a lot.
3. Wires trailing across heat sources. This often happens in the kitchen.
4. wires trailing across floors where people could trip over them. This not only hurts the person who falls but damages the wiring, too!
5. Overloaded sockets. Too many plugs in one socket could overload the wiring and cause a fire (see page14).
6. Power appliances running from lighting circuits. This overloads the wiring too.

Some less obvious problems

Page 10 shows a correctly wired plug. Wiring a plug is an everyday activity – yet one that needs a lot of skill and patience if it is to be done safely! Some attempts will simply not work, or else will 'blow' as soon as they are plugged in. But others would appear to work yet would lead to long-term dangers.

If the live and neutral wires are reversed, the equipment will still work, but could still be 'live' and give a nasty shock – even when switched off! Switches (and fuses, see page 14) must always be in the live wire.

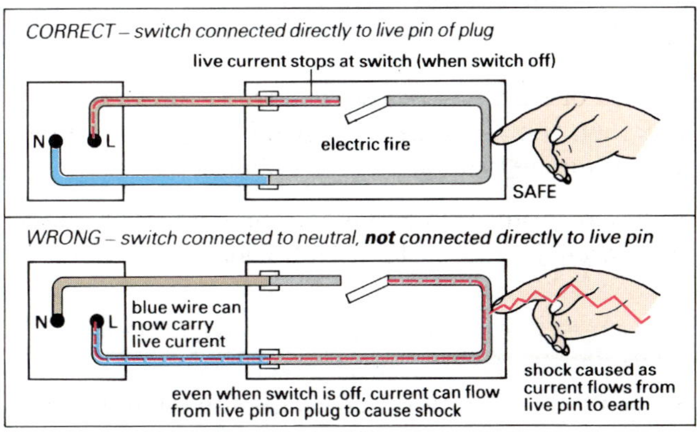

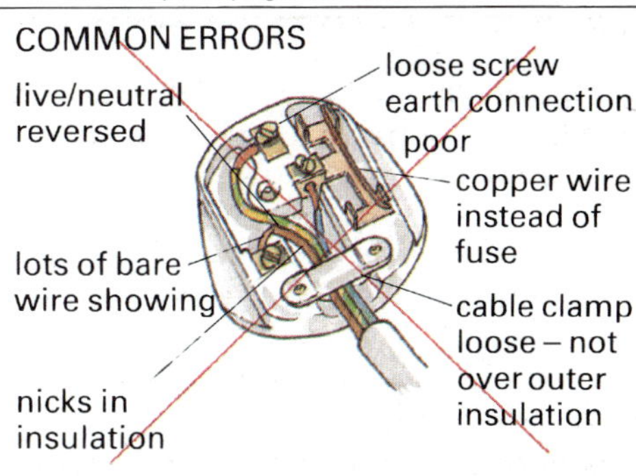

WRONG – AND VERY DANGEROUS

1 Your friends say it doesn't matter if live and neutral wires are reversed. Explain to them why it does.

2 A customer has written to your firm of electricians requesting you to install a power point in his bathroom. Write back and explain why this is not possible.

7 Fuses, circuit breakers and RCDs

Fuses

Plugs have fuses, even stereos have fuses. We know they are for 'safety' and 'protection', but what are they? What do they do? How do they work?

The flow of electricity can make things hot – that's how electric fires and light bulbs work. Fuses also use this principle. A fuse is a wire made of a special metal which, if too much current is passed through, will get hot and melt (or 'fuse'). This then breaks the circuit and so switches off the current – we say that the fuse has 'blown'. Fuse wire can be made to take different, standard currents before melting. The general rule is that thick wire can take a larger current than thin wire. This is because thick wire has more room for electrons to flow, and so has a lower resistance.

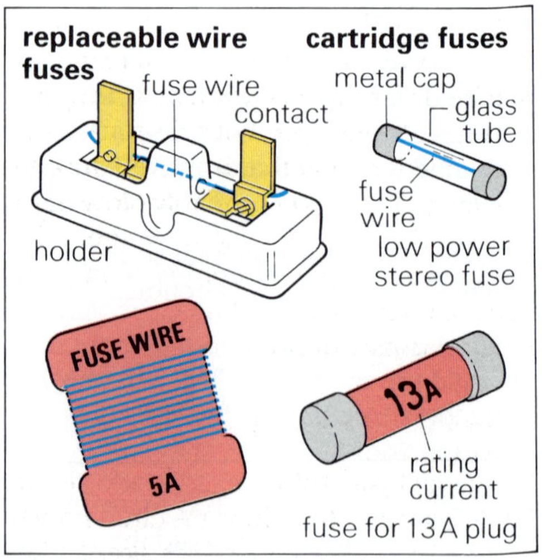

Which fuse?

To choose the correct fuse wire for the job, you need to know the 'working current' of the equipment. A three-bar electric fire can take nearly 13 amperes (13A), so a 5A fuse would blow as soon as the fire was switched on! The rule of thumb is to choose the next standard fuse rating *above* the working current.

	Working current	Fuse
3–bar fire (3 kW)	12.5 A	13 A
hairdrier (750 W)	3 A	5 A
100 W bulb	0.4 A	2 A

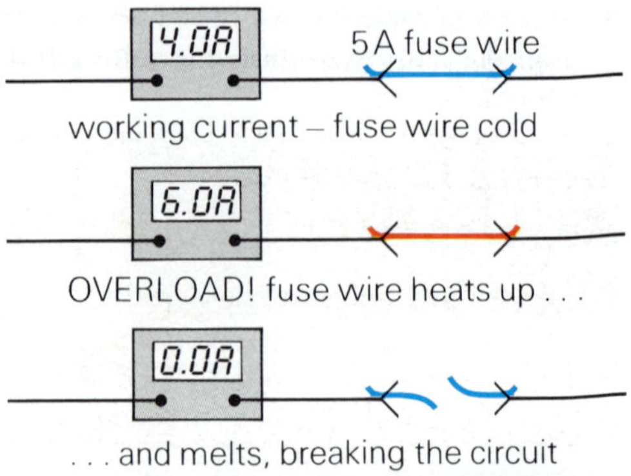

What do they protect?

Fuses melt if overloaded, but they have to heat up first. So if a fault occurs, the delicate electronics in your stereo could be damaged by heat *before* the current was switched off by the fuse. More importantly, fuses react far too slowly to protect you from an electric shock.

Fuses are in fact there to protect the **wiring** in your house. This, too, can get hot if too much current passes through it – hot enough to set fire to the house in extreme cases. That's why you are told not to overload your circuits with lots of adaptors plugged into one socket.

Overloading a socket can lead to fire.

When a house is wired, different sized cables are used for different jobs: thick cables for power circuits, thinner ones for lighting (as bulbs use less current). The problem is that (especially in older houses) people forget and wire new *power* sockets into the old *lighting* circuit! Only the correct fuse can stop overheating and possible fire. So why not just use thick cables for everything? The answer is simple – cost!

Changing fuses

The **cartridge fuses** used in plugs are very easily replaced once the back of the plug has been removed. Household fuses in the **fuse box** are trickier, as a new length of the correct fuse wire must be screwed into the terminals.

Always switch off the current before changing a fuse, and *never* try to replace a fuse with a piece of wire or metal foil – even as a temporary measure. Unless you have discovered and corrected the fault that made the fuse blow in the first place, it will probably blow again. If you were to complete the circuit without a proper fuse, when the power comes on any surge of current could now continue unchecked, causing major damage or fire.

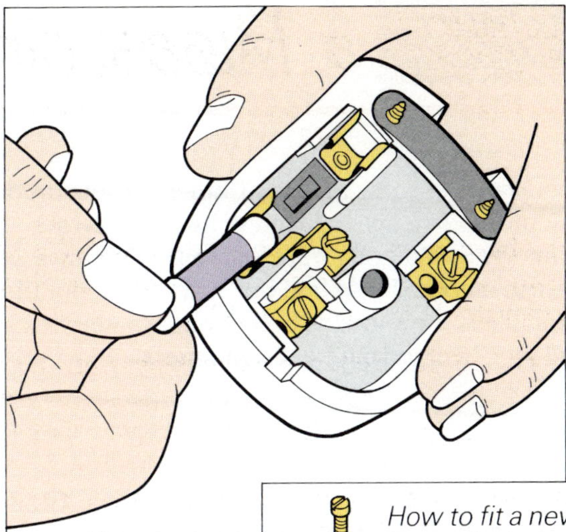

Replacing a cartridge fuse.

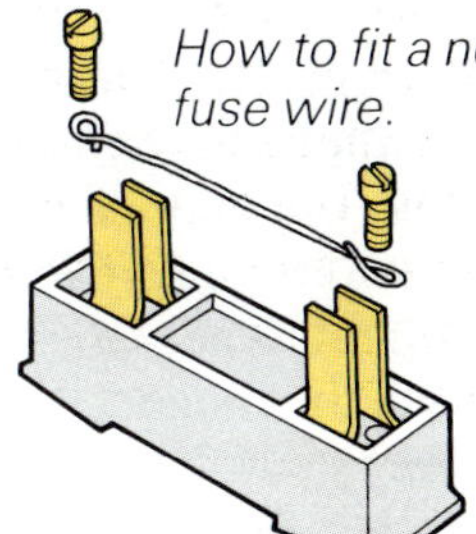

How to fit a new fuse wire.

Circuit breakers . . .

Changing fuses (often in the dark!) is such a fiddly business that they are often now replaced in the fuse box by **circuit breakers**. These don't melt; they use an *electromagnetic* effect (see pages 16–19) to break the circuit if overloaded and, like fuses, come in pre-set 'working current' ratings. Unlike fuses, however, the circuit can be restored at the push of a button.

Industrial circuit breaker.

. . . can be lifesavers!

But, like fuses, circuit breakers are still too slow to save your life. The damage done by a shock depends on the *size* of the current and *how long* it passes for. If only the reaction time of these devices could be reduced enough, electricity could be made totally safe. Now, thanks to microelectronics, it can be done . . .

Normally, the current flowing in the live wire is exactly the same as that in the neutral wire. If a fault occurs, and some of the current flows back through you, however, this balance is upset. **Residual current devices (RCDs)** are designed to detect such an imbalance and to switch off the current within milliseconds – fast enough to save your life!

1 Explain how a fuse will stop a current overload.

2 Which fuse (2 A, 5 A or 13 A) would you fit for:

- **a** 3 kW kettle
- **b** a 100 W stereo
- **c** a 750 W vacuum cleaner?

3 What are fuses designed to protect? What can happen if house wiring is not correctly fused?

4 Describe how RCDs can save your life.

8 Magnets and electromagnets

Thousands of years ago, the Chinese discovered that pieces of a special kind of iron ore always pointed north if hung from a string. Nowadays we use a compass to find our way about, but the principle is the same as both compass needles and pieces of lodestone are **magnets**.

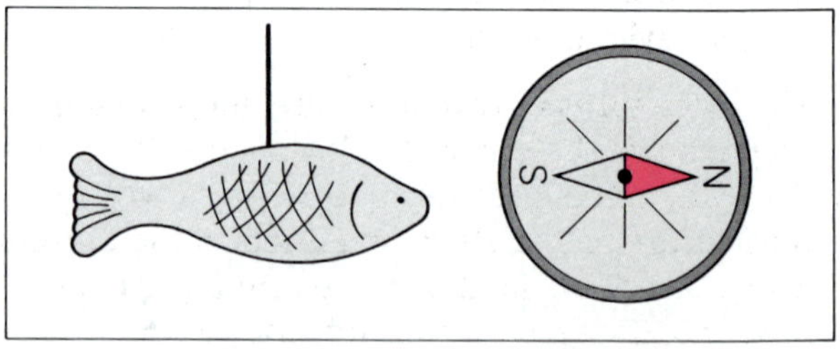

Magnetic tricks

Magnets have many interesting properties. They will pull pieces of iron or steel towards them but do not affect other materials – even other metals, such as copper or aluminium. Also, this force of attraction is not spread out evenly, but is concentrated near the ends, which we call the **poles** of the magnet. You can see this if you dip a magnet into iron filings.

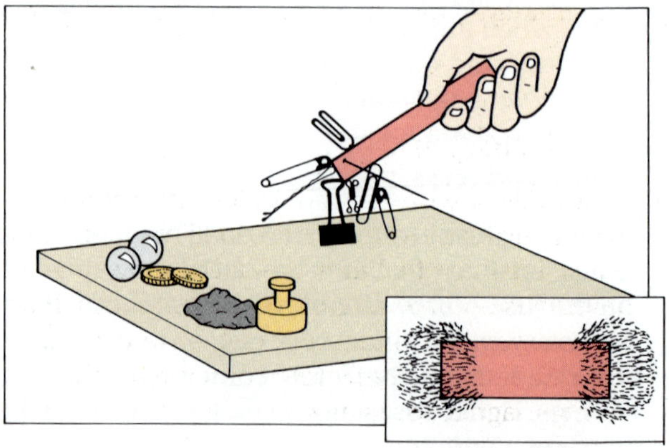

When a magnet is freely suspended, it always comes to rest with the same pole facing north. So this is called the 'north-seeking pole' (or **north pole** for short) and the other is the **south pole**. If the north pole of one magnet is brought near the south pole of another, the two magnets will attract each other. But if two north poles are brought together they push each other away.

The rule is: *like poles repel; unlike poles attract.*

If you have a compass you can use this rule to find which pole of a magnet is which.

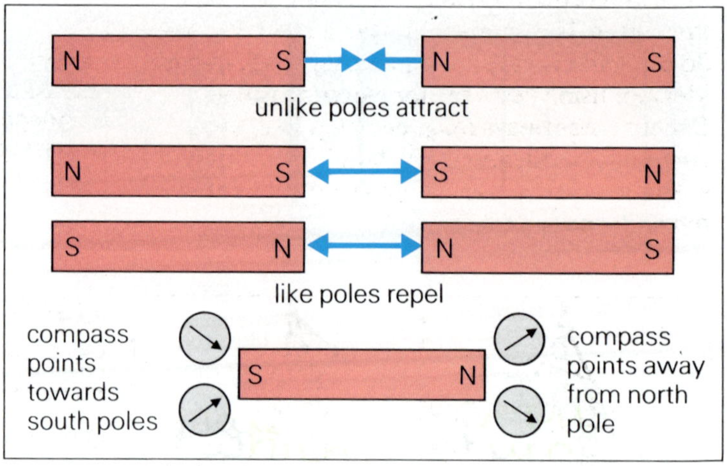

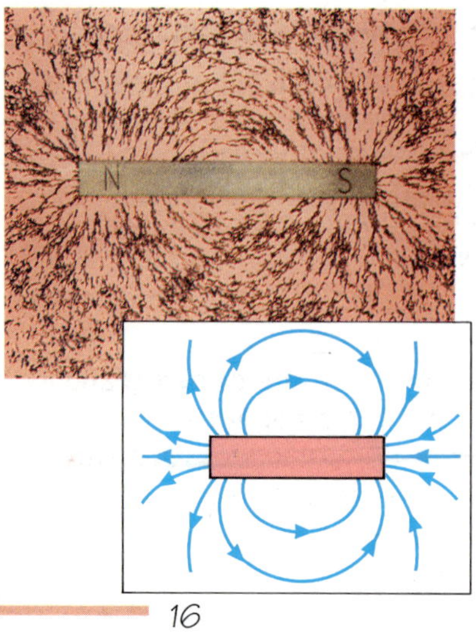

Magnetic fields

All of these things happen because a magnet is surrounded by a **magnetic field**. The pattern of this field can easily be seen if iron filings are shaken around a magnet. In a simplified diagram of this, a series of **lines of force** are marked which show how the north magnetic pole of a small compass would be moved.

The Earth has its own magnetic field, which is why compasses point north! (So what must the *magnetic* polarity of the *geographic* north pole be?)

These **permanent magnets** can be very useful – but they do have their limitations. They can't be made very large and, more importantly, they can't be switched off.

Switchable magnetism

A coil of copper wire will have no effect on a compass needle – until an electric current is passed around it. It then behaves just like a magnet, with poles and a magnetic field.

The more turns of wire there are, the stronger the magnetic field. But it is the flowing electricity, not the wire, that causes this effect. That's why these devices are called **electromagnets**. If the current is increased, the field becomes stronger; if it is reversed, the field is reversed; and, most importantly, if the current is switched off, the field is lost!

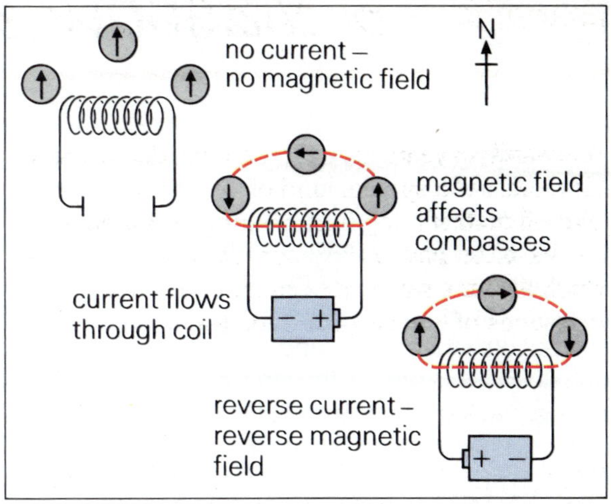

Just add iron

Long coils of wire like this are called **solenoids**. When current flows, their external magnetic field is just like that of a bar magnet. But they also have lines of force running through the coil. If an iron bar is placed inside the coil, it concentrates these lines of magnetic force and makes the electromagnet stronger.

Pure iron does not retain any magnetism when the current is switched off – but a steel bar does. So pure iron is called magnetically 'soft', and is ideal for using as a core for electromagnets. Because steel stays magnetic after being in a solenoid, it is magnetically 'hard'. This means solenoids can be used to make permanent magnets made of steel.

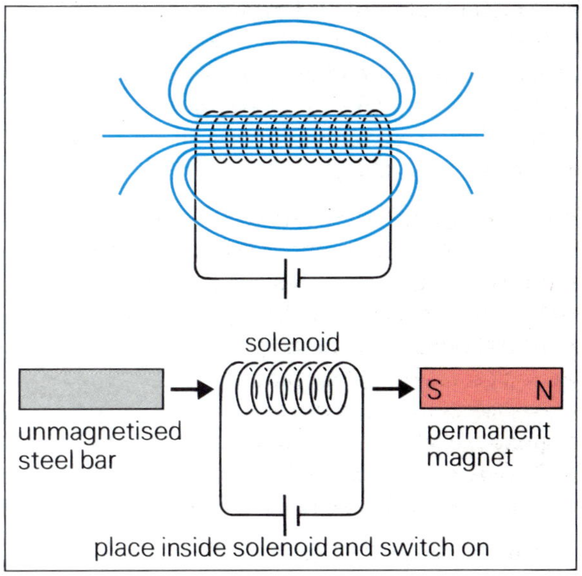

Useful electromagnets

So, electromagnets can be made as strong as you like by:

- increasing the number of coils
- increasing the current
- winding the coils around a 'soft' iron core.

And, most importantly, they can be switched off.

Electromagnets have very many uses, from the 'heavy duty' versions that lift cars in scrapyards to the delicate and complex ones that control the picture on your TV.

1 Give five properties of permanent magnets.

2 What advantages do electromagnets have over permanent ones?

3 **a** Suggest an advantage of being able to turn off an electromagnet.
b Would an electromagnet with a steel core be suitable for such a use? Explain your answer.

9 Electromagnets at work

Buzzers and bells

Electromagnetic 'switchability' is put to good use in electric buzzers and bells. A simple buzzer can be made from a coil, an old nail and a piece of springy steel, as shown. When the circuit is completed, the coil becomes a magnet and so pulls the steel down onto it. But this breaks the circuit! So the steel springs back again, restoring the circuit, and the process is repeated. This continuous 'make and break' causes the steel to vibrate and so a buzz is heard. But if a hammer is connected to the steel spring and a gong is carefully positioned – the buzzer becomes a bell!

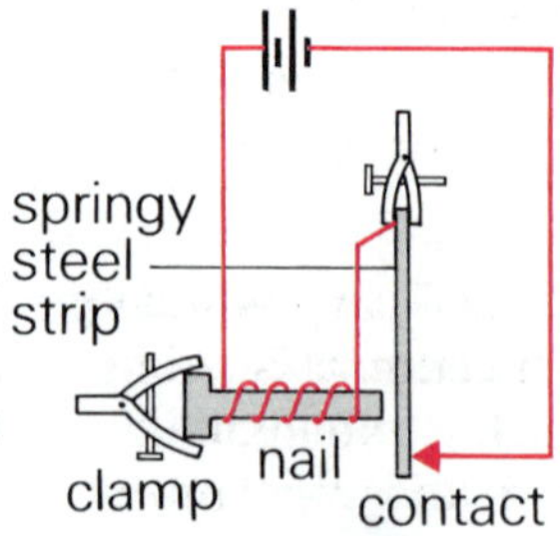

simple buzzer

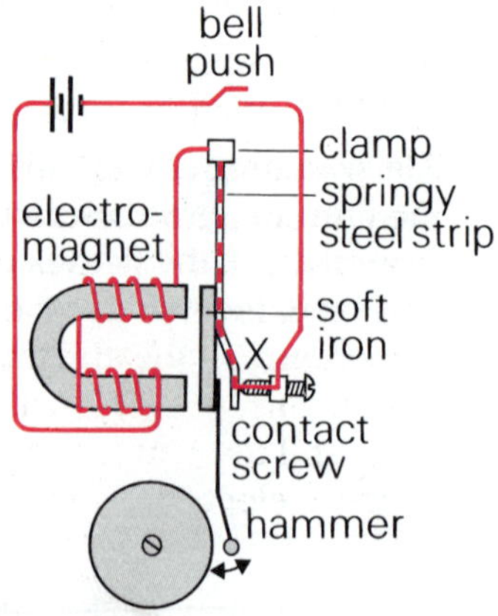

bell

Relays

Electromagnetic effects can also be used to throw switches. In a **relay**, the electromagnet pulls down an iron plate which, in turn, pushes two electrical contacts together. This 'switching at a distance' can be very useful – it once formed the basis of our automatic telephone exchanges.

A relay device can also save money when making cars. The starter motor of a car takes a very high current (up to 100 A), so it needs very thick cables – which are very expensive. One way of starting the car would be to run thick cables to carry a high current from the battery to the ignition key switch to the starter motor – using a lot of expensive cable! A cheaper way is shown in the diagram – this uses thin, low-current wires to energise a relay, which *then* switches on the high current needed by the starter. All that is now needed is a short, thick wire from the positive terminal of the battery. (Cars employ the sneaky trick of using the metal body of the car to complete the circuit! This is called an **earth return**.)

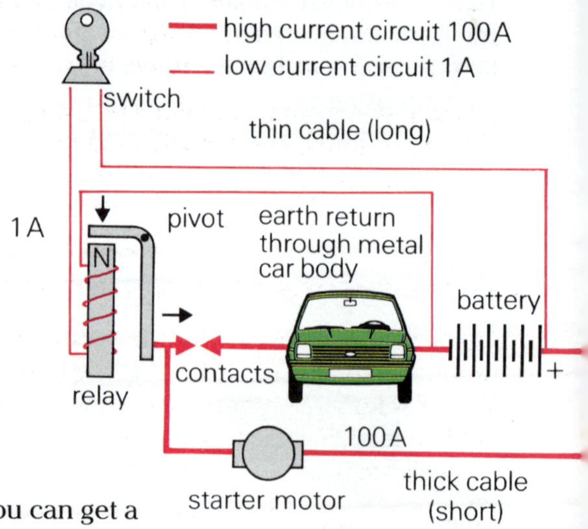

Move and measure

If you put an electromagnet next to a permanent magnet, you can get a force of attraction or repulsion, just as you can with two permanent magnets. By using an electromagnet, you can reverse the effect by reversing the current in the coil. You can also increase the force by increasing the number of coils in the electromagnet, or by increasing the current.

This last effect is used to measure current in a **moving coil** electrical meter. Here, current flowing through a flat coil forms an electromagnet, which tries to turn in a magnetic field. The coil is also attached to a spring – small turns need only a small force, but large turns need a larger force. The greater the current in the coil, the more it turns. This movement can be made to move a pointer across a scale.

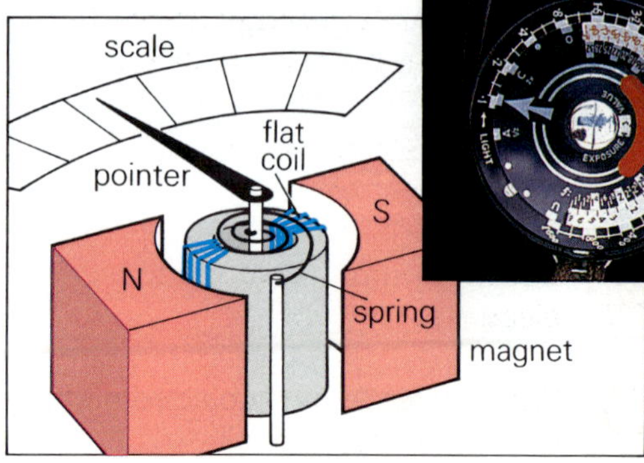

In a spin

Coils will only turn in a magnetic field until they are 'lined up' with it. But the direction in which the coil turns depends on the direction of the current. If you could reverse the current just at the critical moment, you could make the coil continue to turn . . .

Electric motors work in just this way, switching the current automatically. The current is fed in through carbon brushes which make contact with metal half-rings. These reverse the current in the coil every half turn. In commercial motors many turns of wire are used around a soft iron core, and the permanent magnets are replaced by more electromagnets to give a stronger field.

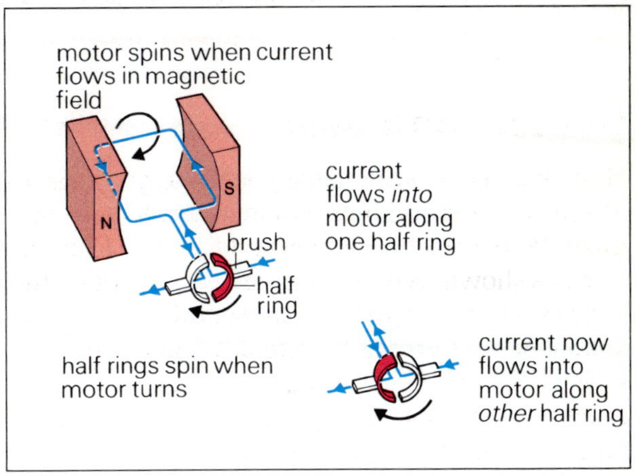

Diagrams show how an electric motor works.

Generating electricity

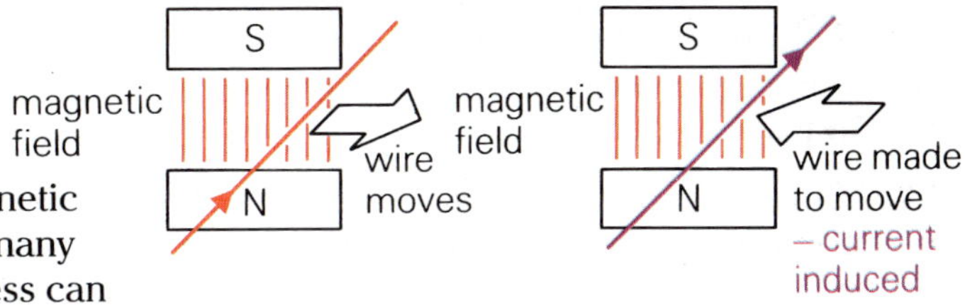

In a motor, electrical energy is turned into kinetic energy – the energy of motion. But, as with many **transducers** or 'energy changers', this process can be reversed. In its simplest form, a wire carrying a current through a magnetic field will be moved. But if you move a wire through a field, an electric current will be **induced** – made to flow – in it.

A larger effect can be obtained by using a coil with many turns. And it doesn't matter if it's the magnet or the coil that moves – so long as there is movement!

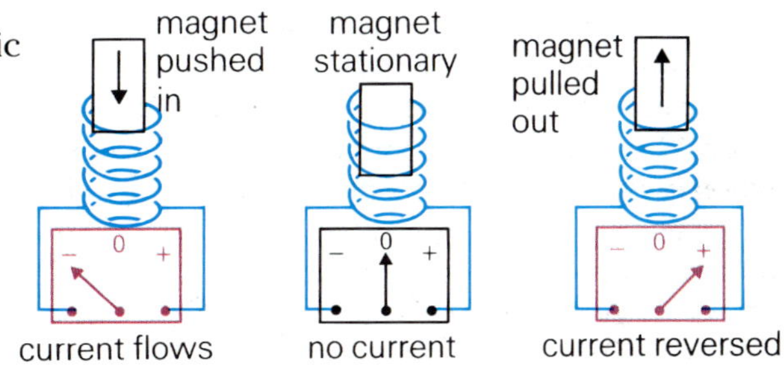

Generators and dynamos

These simple effects would not be suitable for the large-scale production of electricity. Real **generators and dynamos** use a similar set-up to a motor, with a coil spinning in an electromagnetic field. Indeed, if you connect a motor to an ammeter and spin its coil, you will see just how reversible these transducers are!

An interesting point is that the current induced in the coil in this way flows backwards and forwards with every turn – mimicking the current reversal needed to keep a motor turning. This type of current is called **alternating current** (a.c.) and you are quite used to using it . . . as mains electricity (see page 10).

1 How can electromagnets be made stronger?

2 Describe, step by step, how an electric bell works.

3 Why is it an advantage to use a relay on a car starter motor?

4 How is the coil in an electric motor made to keep turning?

5 How can a motor be turned into a generator? What type of current is produced?

10 Electromagnetism and sound

Sound vibrations

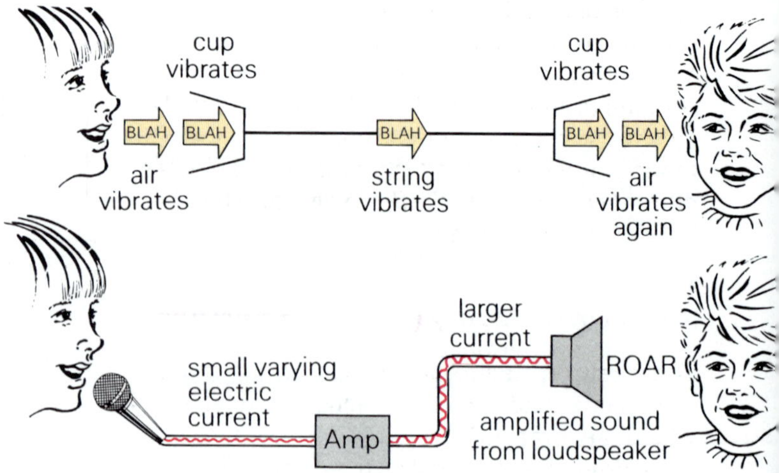

Have you ever made a string telephone? This works because the sounds we hear travel along the strings as bursts of vibrations. In the same way, we hear each other talking because the sound vibrations we make as we speak travel through the air to the listener.

Public address (PA) systems and telephones use the same basic idea but, rather than having a vibrating string, the vibrations are turned into a varying electric current by a **microphone**. This is then turned back to sound vibrations by a **loudspeaker** at the other end. The advantage of this system is that the electrical signal may be amplified to make it louder (or travel further). How is this done?

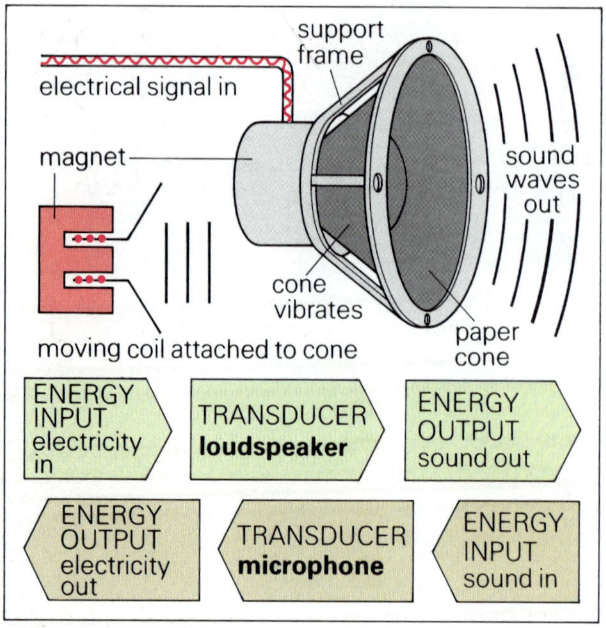

Microphones and loudspeakers

These are **transducers** or energy convertors. Microphones turn sound energy into electrical energy. Moving-coil microphones have a coil of wire set in a magnetic field. Sound vibrations make this coil move, generating a varying electric current by **electromagnetic induction**, like a small-scale generator. The pattern of the varying current matches the pattern of the sound waves. Loudspeakers turn electrical energy into sound energy. Moving-coil loudspeakers are very similar, but work in reverse. The varying current is fed into a coil in a magnetic field. This causes the coil to vibrate by a motor effect. The coil is attached to a paper cone, and this causes the air to vibrate, giving off sound waves again.

Telephones

These use a different system of transducers. In the mouthpiece microphone, a current is made to flow through a box of carbon granules. Sound waves squash this box, changing the resistance of the granules and so giving a varying current. In the earpiece, the varying current is fed into an electromagnet. This makes a springy steel plate vibrate, generating sound waves again.

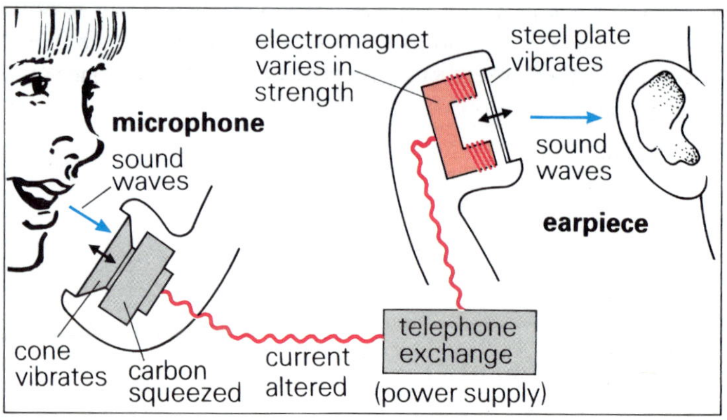

Recording sound

Early sound recording techniques simply used the mechanical vibrations of sound to scratch grooves onto a disc. The sound was then replayed by running a needle along the groove. You can still get sound out of a record in this way (but make sure it's an old and unwanted one!) Modern systems are much more sophisticated though, and convert the vibrations to an electric current *electromagnetically*, to give greater control over the sound.

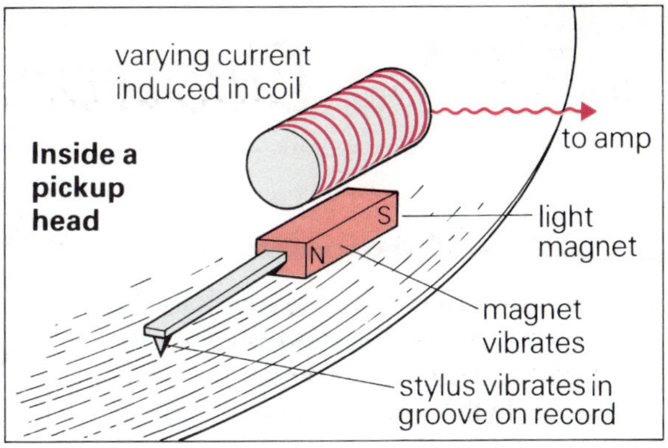

Tape and cassette recorders

These rely on electromagnetism too. The tape used has a coating of tiny magnetic particles, which are arranged randomly at first. During **recording**, the electrical signal carrying the sound pattern is passed to an electromagnet in the tape head. This produces a varying magnetic field, which lines up the magnetic particles. During **playback**, the magnetic pattern passes over the tape head, inducing a similarly varying current in the coil. This is then fed to the amplifier and on to the loudspeaker.

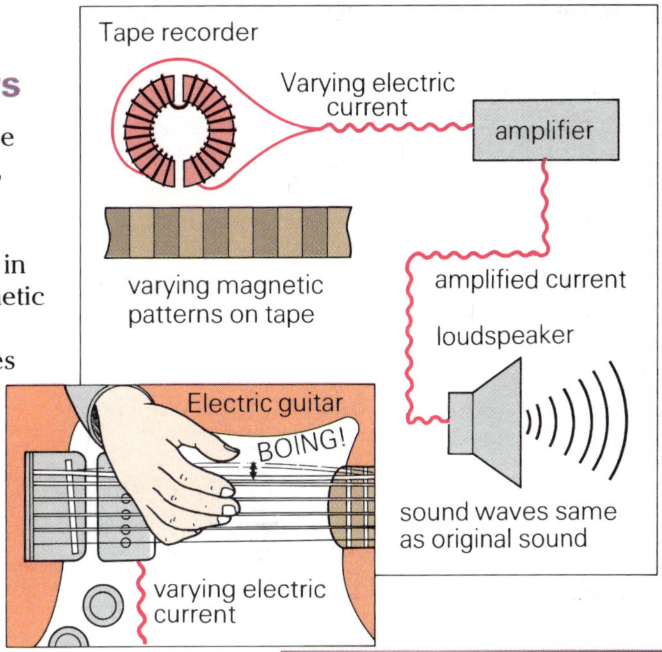

Making music electromagnetically

Electric guitars are really electromagnetic guitars! The vibrating metal strings induce a current in the pickup coils, which is then passed on to the amplifier.

The electromagnetic TV!

Black and White TVs work by firing a beam of electrons at the screen, which glows where they strike. Complex electromagnets and high voltage plates are used to make this beam move across and down the screen so fast that your eye can't keep up with it. At the same time, a varying signal from the aerial (or your video) makes the beam seem stronger or weaker. As your eye retains an image for as long as the beam takes to scan the entire screen, you see a complete picture! Colour TVs are similar but more complicated.

Caught in the act.

1. Terry said he 'bugged' his brother's room by plugging the wires from the extension speaker that was in there into the input at the stereo. Could he have done this? Explain your answer.

2. Describe the differences between a telephone mouthpiece and a moving coil microphone.

3. Describe briefly and in your own words how **a** a record player, **b** a cassette recorder and **c** an electric guitar work.

4. The TV picture shown above was taken with a very fast exposure camera. Explain why it looks like it does.

11 Charges at work

Creating static charges

Static charges (which you learned about earlier) can build up on insulators if they are rubbed together. Some materials, such as nylon or polythene, tend to pick up extra electrons and so become *negatively* charged. Others, such as ebony or glass, tend to lose electrons and so become *positively* charged.

If similarly charged rods are brought together, they repel each other, while oppositely charged rods attract each other. The rule is: *like charges repel; unlike charges attract*.

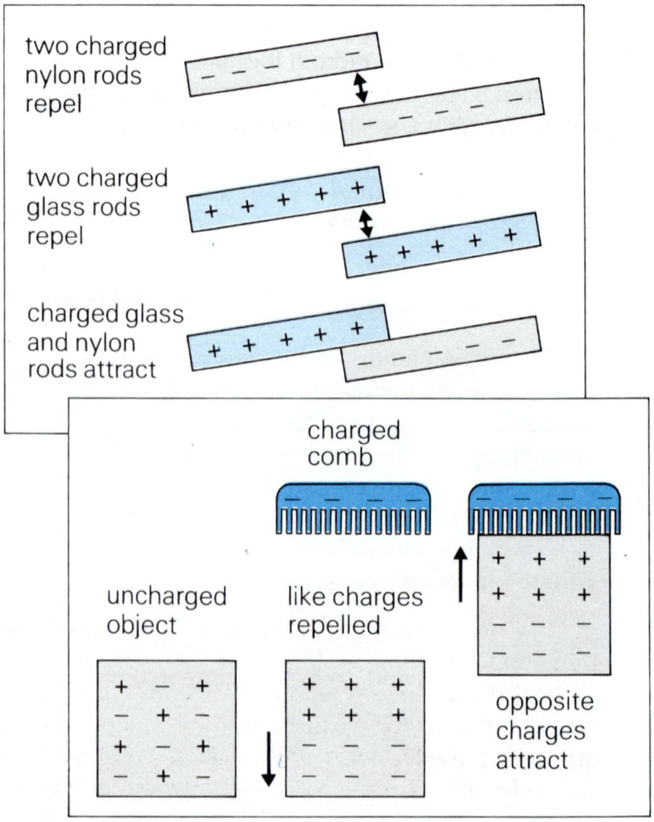

How can a comb pick up a paper?

A freshly rubbed comb will pick up pieces of paper, and a rubbed balloon will stick to a wall. So what makes these rubbed (charged) objects attract uncharged ones?

You need to remember that *everything* contains electric charges, but usually they are in balance. When a charged object is brought near, however, this balance can be upset enough to allow attraction to occur.

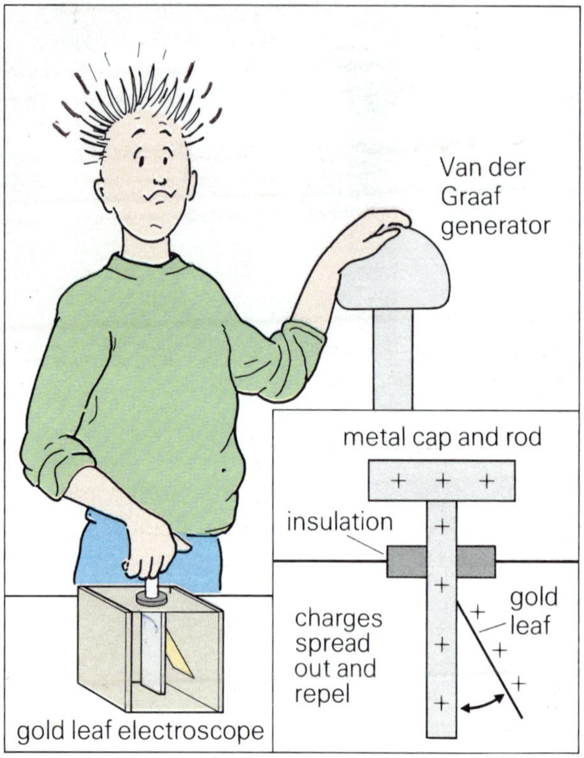

Useful static repulsion

You may have seen experiments using a machine called a Van der Graaf generator, which can build up very large electrostatic charges. If a volunteer stands on an insulated plate and puts a hand on the charge dome, he or she will get a very hair-raising experience!

This happens because the charge spreads out all over the surface of the body and every single hair gets the same charge, and so *pushes away* its neighbour. This idea is put to work in electrostatic paint-spraying. Here, every droplet of paint gets the same charge and so keeps apart from its neighbour, giving a very smooth spray and finish.

Repulsion effects can also be used to detect charges. In a gold leaf electroscope, a thin strip of gold leaf is attached to a metal bar in an insulated box. If the cap is charged, this charge spreads out and causes the gold leaf to rise by electrostatic repulsion.

Making static flow

The charged dome of a Van der Graaf generator will spark to Earth – through you if you get too close! It can easily be made to discharge to Earth through a wire and a neon tube – making the tube light up as the charge flows to Earth. A current can be detected in the wire by any sensitive meter. Why? Don't forget that current electricity is just flowing electrical charge!

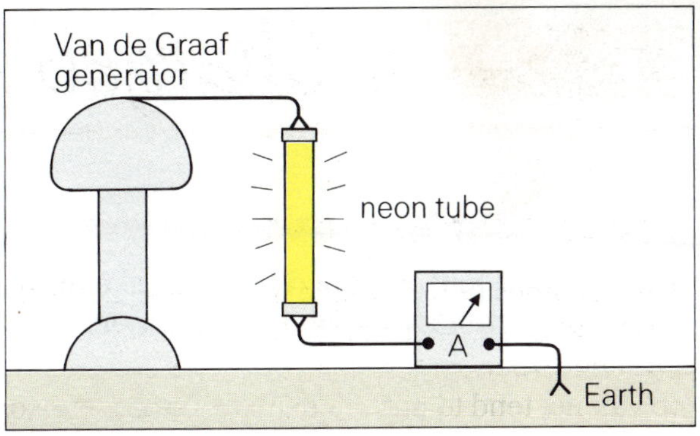

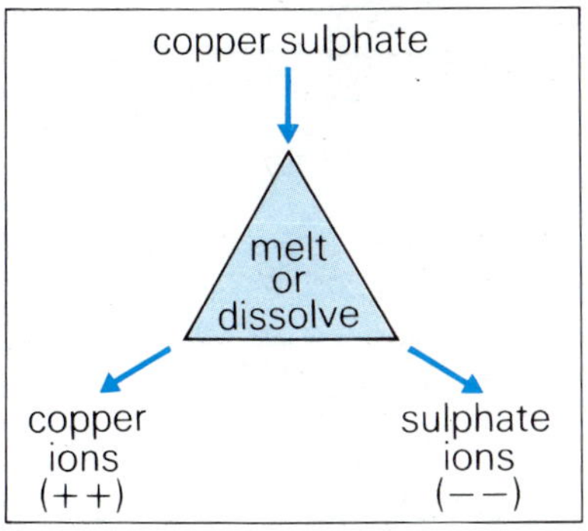

Using current to overcome static

Many compounds of metals are **ionic**. That means they are made up of positively charged bits and negatively charged bits that are held together by electrostatic attraction. (Charged particles are called **ions**.) If these compounds are melted or dissolved in water, however, these ions separate and may be torn apart by a direct current in a process called **electrolysis**.

Electroplating

If two wires are connected to a d.c. source and dipped into copper sulphate solution, the negative wire (the **cathode**) gets coated with fresh, metallic copper. This is because the copper in the solution has a positive charge and so is pulled towards the negative cathode. Here, the extra electrons cancel out the charge on the copper ions, and a **plating** of metallic copper is deposited on the cathode. Various other metal **electroplatings** can be made if you carry out electrolysis of the right solutions.

An electric current is just a flow of electrons: the larger the current and/or the longer you leave it flowing, the more metal you get from the solution. This method is used in industry to purify copper by electrolysis.

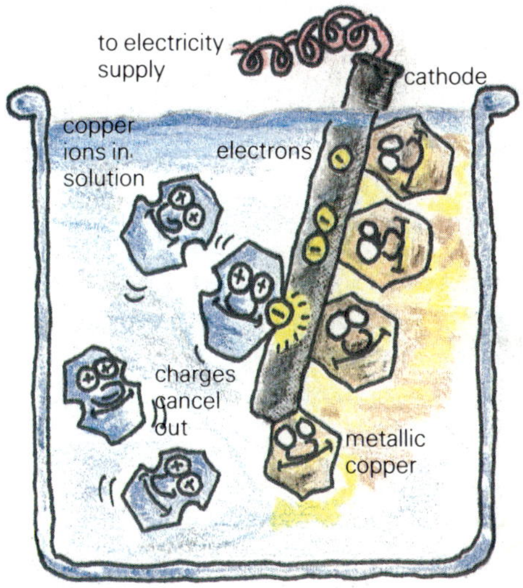

Electrolysis – using electricity to separate metals from their compounds

Not always an easy solution

Aluminium is too reactive to get from solution, but it is produced industrially by the electrolysis of its molten ore. Unfortunately, the high melting point of its ore means that vast amounts of electricity are needed first to melt and then tear it from its ore. Because of this, aluminium manufacturers need their own power stations – and prefer to use cheap hydro-electric power, where electricity is generated from flowing water nearby.

1 What feature of static electricity is similar to a feature of magnetism?

2 How could you show that static electricity can have the same effect as current electricity?

3 Find out three different metals which are used for electroplating. Give a use for each one of your electroplated metal coatings.

4 Aluminium was only discovered in 1825. Why do you think this is so?

12 Measuring electricity

Mastering the units

You've read about amps and volts but, like many people, you may still be rather muddled and confused about them. So what is the difference?

Amps flow . . .

We use **amps** or amperes (A) as a measure of the *rate of flow* of electric current – the number of units of charge which pass every second. (The standard unit of charge is called a **coulomb**.)

low current

high current

To use a water model again, compare a waterfall in winter flood to the same waterfall as a summer trickle. The height of the fall is the same, the speed at which the water falls is the same. The only difference is the rate of flow – the amount falling every second.

. . . volts hurt!

We use **volts** (V), on the other hand, as a measure of the amount of *energy* carried by each unit of charge. This tells us how much work can be done by the current.

In a water model, compare the energy and possible effects of a bucket of water tipped from the top of a door to one dropped from the top of a skyscraper! So the number of volts tell us about the 'push' on the electrons, or the 'kick' of energy that they carry – or, on you, how much they hurt!

low voltage

high voltage

current and voltage go up and down together!

the resistance/ current see saw

How does resistance fit in?

In simple circuits, *the relative size of the current flowing depends on the resistance*. A low resistance will allow a high current to flow, while a high resistance will allow only a low current to flow – a sort of see-saw (*inverse*) relationship.

But in a given circuit, *the actual size of the current also depends on the voltage*. In this case, however, the current rises as the voltage rises and falls as it falls – a more *direct* relationship.

The resistance of a circuit is measured in **ohms** (Ω) – it is calculated by dividing the voltage by the current.

Circuits

In a simple circuit there is just one loop, so the flow of electrons (the current) is the same all the way around it. This is called a **series** circuit.

Another common type of circuit has two or more separate branches. Like a river splitting and flowing around an island, the current in the main wire is split between the branches, only to recombine before returning to the 'pump'. This is called a **parallel** circuit.

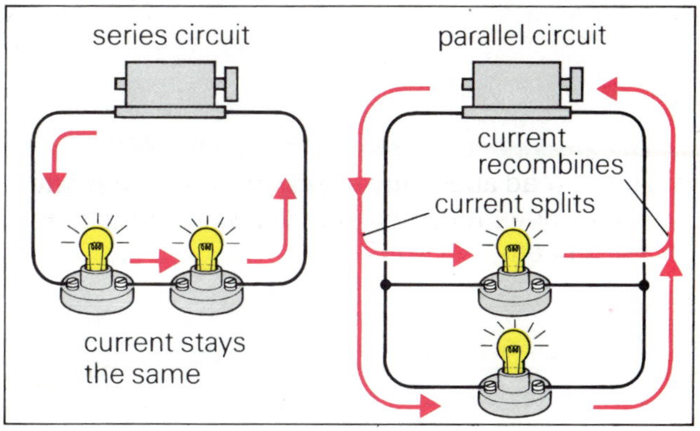

ammeter in series

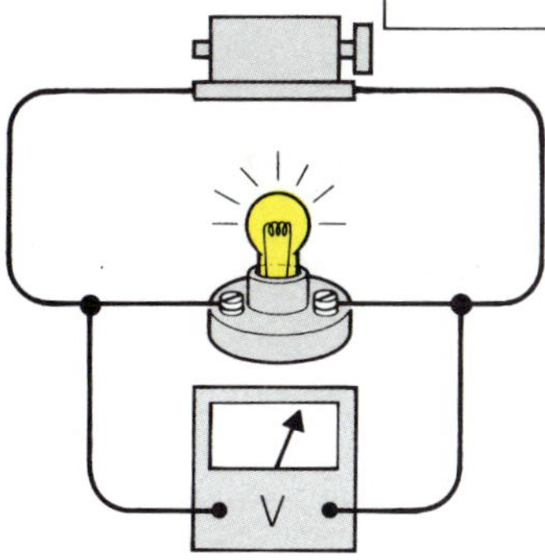

voltmeter in parallel

Measuring

Current is measured using an **ammeter**. A circuit must be broken and the ammeter put in, in *series*, to measure current, as *all* the current must flow through the meter.

Voltage is measured with a **voltmeter**. Voltage readings are easier to take, however, as the voltmeter leads need only be connected in *parallel* across the points to be tested.

Energy and how to pay for it

The energy flowing through an electric circuit depends on the *voltage*, the *current* – and *how long it has been flowing!* This can be measured directly using a **joulemeter**, which fits into the circuit in series like an ammeter.

You pay for electricity at home by how much energy you have used – you have a 'meter' permanently wired into the circuit which the Electricity Company come to read every three months or so. Scientists use the **joule** to measure energy, but this is rather small for household use. Your meter at home measures in **kilowatt hour** 'units', where 1 unit equals 3.6 million joules and costs you about 7p (at the time this book was printed).

You probably have an electrictity meter like this at home.

1. Explain, in words, the difference between current (in amps) and voltage (in volts). Think up your own models to help you.

2. Try to describe, in words, the relationships between current, voltage and resistance.

3. How do series circuits and parallel circuits differ? Draw diagrams and give examples.

4. Describe how you would practically measure voltage and current.

13 Clever tricks with a.c.

The amount of **power** used by an electrical circuit is found by *multiplying the voltage and the current*. So the same amount of power could be delivered by:

- high voltage and low current, or
- low voltage and high current.

Sometimes we need high voltage, sometimes high current – wouldn't it be useful if we could change from one to the other? With a.c. we can – using a **transformer**.

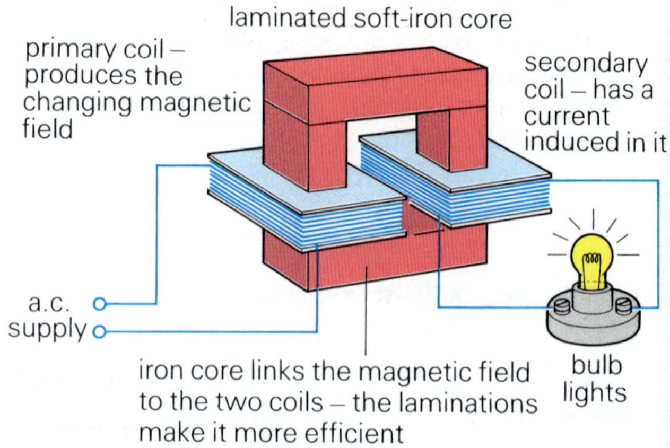

How transformers work

On page 19 it was described how an electric current is produced in a generator, by moving a coil in a magnetic field – with the magnetic field staying constant all the time. But exactly the same effect can be obtained if the coil stays still and the field moves.

Pass a direct current through a coil and it becomes an electromagnet, with a magnetic field from its north to south pole. But pass a.c. through a coil and this field must switch backwards and forwards as the current reverses.

Put these ideas together and what do you have? A transformer!

Transforming voltages up and down

The strength of an electromagnet is controlled by the number of turns of wire. The effect of a transformer depends on the ratio of the *number of turns in the primary and secondary coils*. If the secondary coil has four times more turns than the primary coil, the voltage from the secondary coil will be four times greater. If the number of coils were four times less, the voltage would be reduced down by a factor of four.

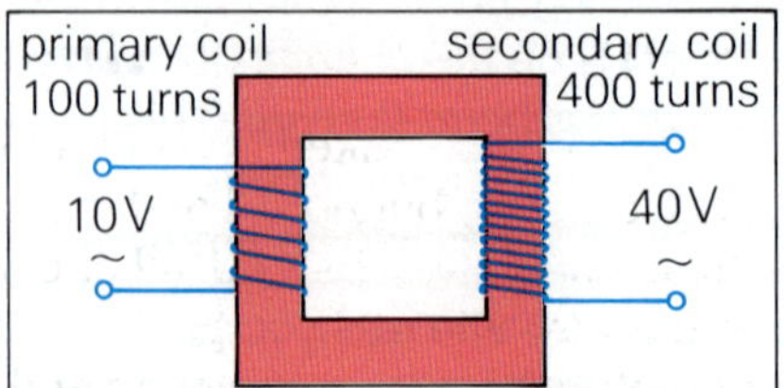

step-up (ratio 1:4)

$$\frac{\text{voltage in secondary}}{\text{voltage in primary}} = \frac{\text{no. of turns in secondary}}{\text{no. of turns in primary}}$$

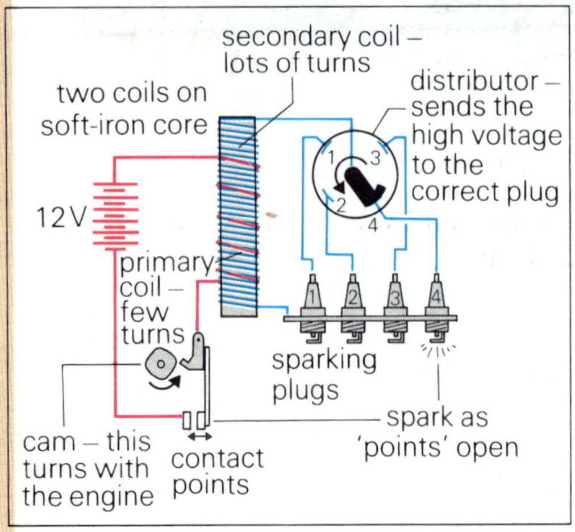

'Step-up' and spark

In a petrol engine, a high voltage is needed to make a **spark** to ignite the petrol/air mixture. Yet cars only have 12V d.c. batteries . . .

The answer is to use a **step-up transformer** – often just called the 'coil' in a car. As transformers will not work with continuous d.c. (as the field does not move once it is 'on'), the circuit must be switched on and off automatically. This can be done by opening **contact 'points'** in the low-voltage 12V primary circuit, in time with the spin of the engine. As the 'points' open, the magnetic field changes (collapses to zero). A high voltage is momentarily generated by the changing field, and this is passed to each spark plug in turn by the **distributor**.

'Step-down' and heat-up

Heating effects are most efficient at the 'high current' end of the power see-saw. Electric welders use a **step-down transformer** which has just a few, thick wire turns in the secondary coil to produce a very high current.
If this short circuits across pieces of metal, the heat produced is great enough to cause local melting, welding the pieces together.

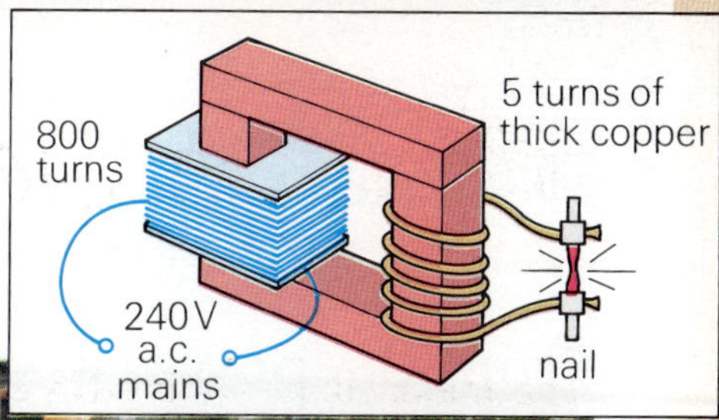

Welding in progress during the assembly of concrete mixers.

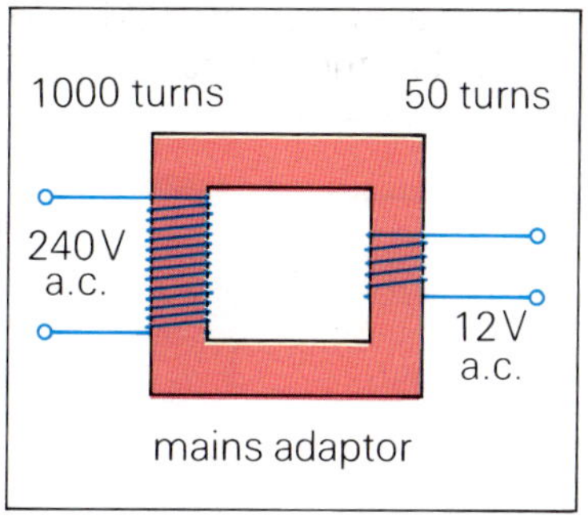

Step-down and boogie!

Modern electronic equipment such as stereos, radios and computers, run on low-voltage d.c. supplies. These can be provided from batteries but, as those of you with portable cassette players will know, batteries soon run out and are expensive to replace. Mains electricity is much cheaper.

Mains adaptors can be used either built-in or separate from most electronic equipment. These adaptors use a step-down transformer to reduce the mains voltage to a suitable low voltage. (The overall power is kept low by having thin, higher-resistance wires in the transformer, to limit the size of the current.) But this is still a.c., so something else must be done . . .

Semi-conductor diodes

So far we have talked of conductors, insulators and resistors, but not all materials fit neatly into these categories. Indeed, all of our transistor and microchip technology depends on a group of materials, including silicon and germanium, which have much more complex properties and are known as **semi-conductors**.

One of the simplest semi-conductor devices is the **diode**. This lets current flow in *one* direction, but acts as an insulator if the voltage is *reversed*. Diodes can therefore be used as one-way valves, to protect equipment from an accidentally reversed voltage that might otherwise damage it.

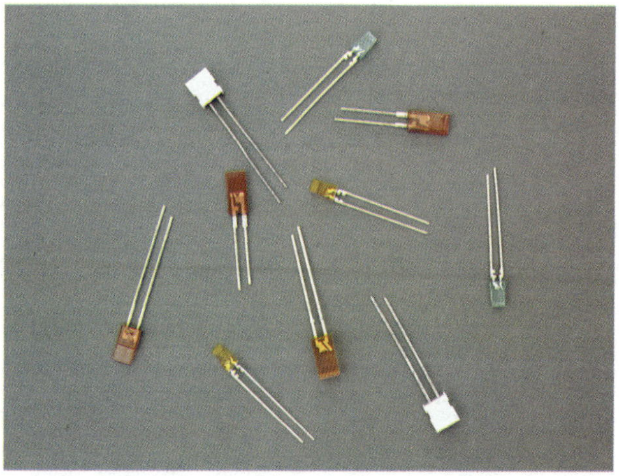

A selection of modern electronics diodes.

This one-way effect can also be used to turn a.c. to d.c. – so you'll also find diodes in any mains adaptor. If you want to know more you'll have to read a book on electronics!

1. Compare the way a transformer works with what happens in a generator.
2. What is a step-up transformer? How is it used in a car?
3. What is a step-down transformer? How is it used in an electric welder?
4. What are diodes? How do they:
   a protect equipment
   b change a.c. to d.c.?

14 Plugging into electricity

From the power station . . .

Power stations are energy converters (transducers).

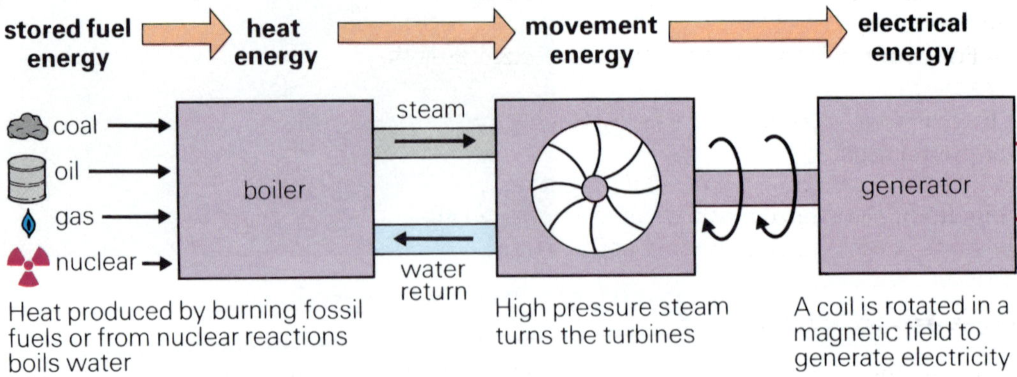

. . . through the National Grid . . .

All the electricity that is supplied by the power stations is fed into the 'energy highway' that spans the country – the **National Grid**. This allows regional variations in supply and demand to be balanced out. (For more information, see the Energy module, spread 4).

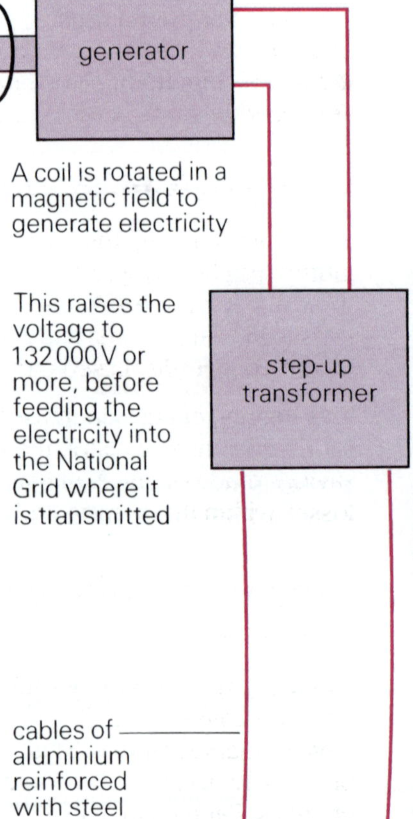

. . . into step-down transformers . . .

These step the voltage down to suitable working levels – sometimes several thousand volts for industry, but always 240V for the home. Some energy is lost in these transformers: if you live near one that 'hums' a lot you can listen in to this wasted energy!

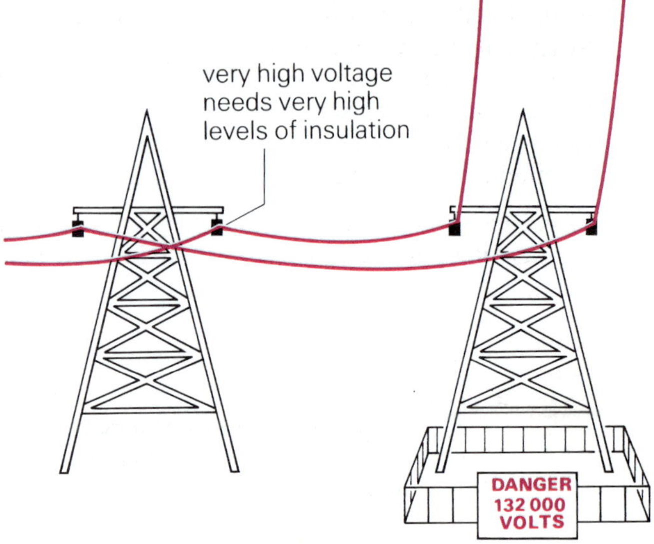

. . . for everyone to use

In this country nearly everyone makes use of electricity for lighting at home and at work. Many people use it for cooking, heating and thousands of different types of electrical equipment. There are many specialist uses:

- *Manufacturing* – Extracting and refining various metals; powering robots to make cars.
- *Transport* – Electric motors in London Underground trains; various railway trains.
- *Business* – For communications and computers (such as in the Stock Exchange).
- *Leisure* – Floodlights at sporting events; power for video games and for fairground rides.
- *Broadcasting* – Transmitting radio and TV programmes.
- *Health* – Monitoring life-support machines in intensive care.
- *Education* – Computers . . . and school bells!

Why such high voltage?

The cables carrying the current through the National Grid are thick and made of aluminium (a very good conductor). However, their great length (several thousand kilometers) means that altogether they do have a significant resistance. This means that some energy will be lost owing to the electrical heating effect (discussed earlier in this module).

This heating effect is increased dramatically as the current increases, so it is far more efficient to transmit the power at high voltage/low current. The energy savings made on the National Grid as a whole by doing this far outweigh energy losses within the step-up and step-down transformers.

Why is electricity so expensive?

Electricity is a secondary source of energy – unlike coal, oil or gas, we have to manufacture it. This process involves many energy changes. Each change uses up a little bit of the energy, with the result that the overall system 'wastes' nearly two-thirds of its energy. Even then, there are further losses in the National Grid itself. No wonder electricity is expensive!

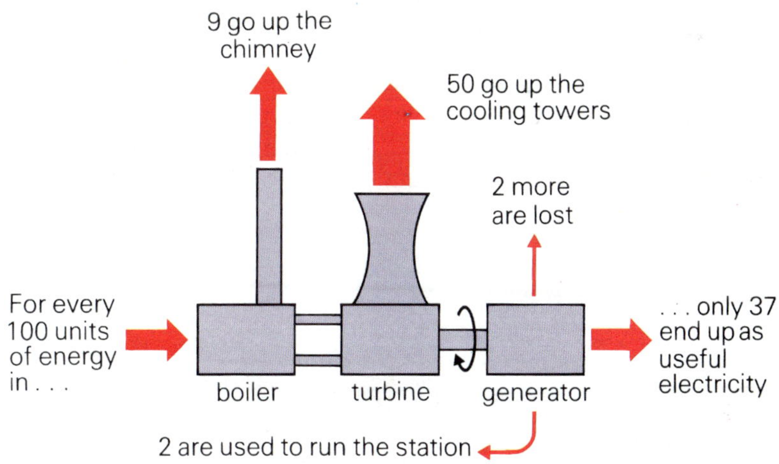

As you can see, electricity is 'Big Business', affecting nearly every aspect of our lives. We take it for granted – but could you imagine life without it?

1

a What do you think are the five biggest advantages of having electricity? In each case how could people cope if there was no electricity?

b What do you think are the five disadvantages of electricity?

c Explain if you think the advantages outweigh the disadvantages.

15 For you to do

1 Angie set up a circuit to test whether different things conducted electricity or not. A piece of copper made the bulb light up.

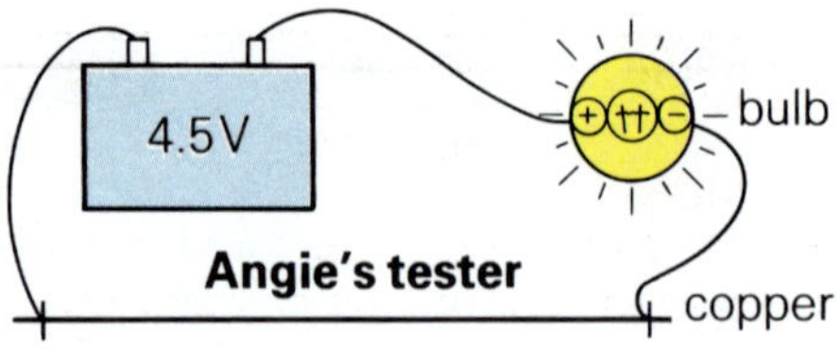

a Is copper a conductor or insulator?

b Would the bulb light up if the copper was replaced by:

i	a penny	iv	a matchstick
ii	a gold ring	v	a rubber
iii	a plastic comb	vi	an iron nail?

2 **a** Denzil set up a circuit as shown. His paper-clip switch had three positions, A, B and C.

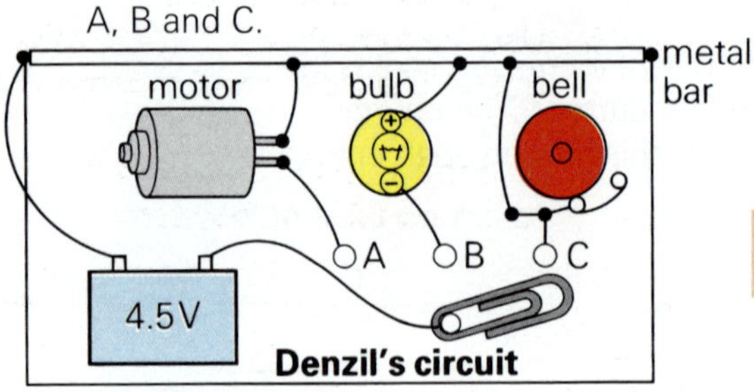

Which position would:

i ring the bell

ii spin the motor

iii light the bulb?

b Freda set up a circuit using a battery, a buzzer, three lengths of wire with crocodile clips and a switch. The buzzer came on only when the switch was turned on. Draw a picture of her circuit.

3 Which of the energy changers shown below is designed most efficiently to change:

a electricity to sound

b motion to electricity

c electricity to motion

d electricity to light

e chemical energy to electricity?

Energy changers: lightbulb, battery, electric motor, microphone, loudspeaker, dynamo.

4 Which circuit diagram below could represent:

a a simple torch

b a light with a dimmer switch

c a two-bar fire with separate switches

d a variable-speed motor

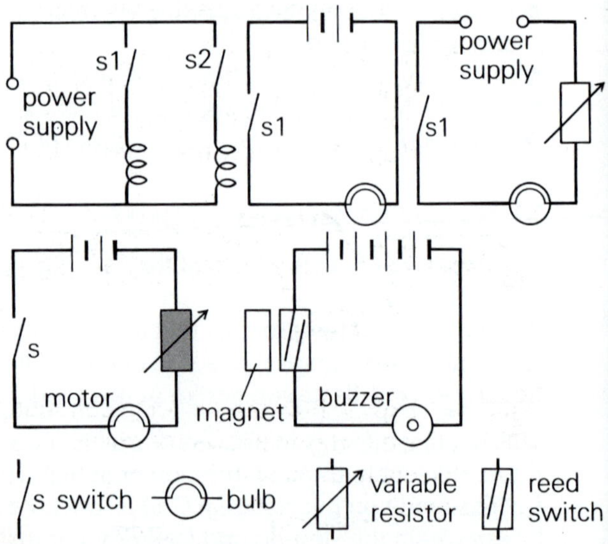

5 If two cells make each of the two bulbs glow to 'standard brightness', would the bulbs in the circuits shown glow brighter, the same, dimmer, or not at all?

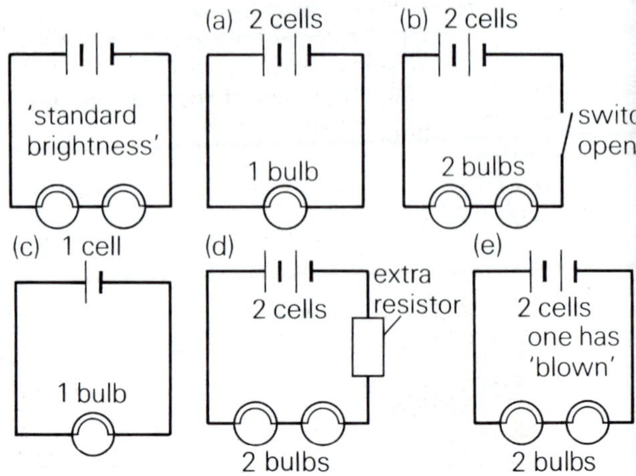

6 An electromagnet can be made from coils of wire connected to a d.c. power supply.

a Suggest three ways to make a simple electromagnet stronger.

b What happens to the magnetic field if:

i the current is switched off

ii the current is reversed?

7 **a** If current is passed along a wire in a magnetic field, a force acts on the wire which can make it move.

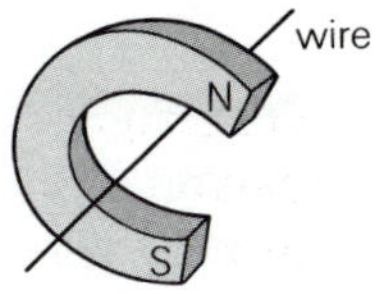

What happens to this force if:

i the current is increased

ii the magnetic field is reversed?

b If a direct current is passed through a coil of wire in a magnetic field as shown, what will happen to it? (Draw a diagram to show how it ends up.)

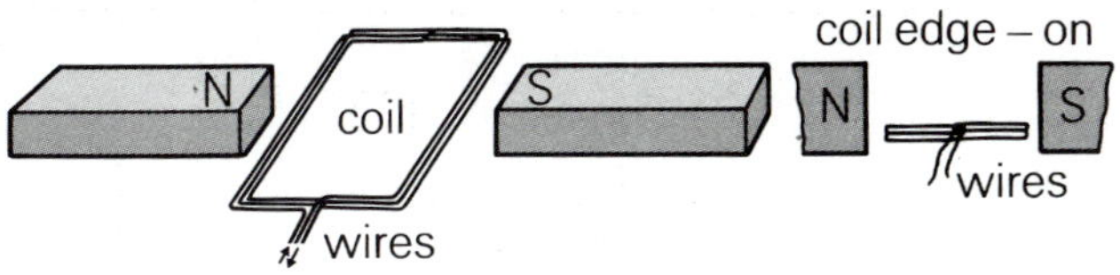

8 **a** Explain how the split-ring commutor in a d.c. motor allows the coil to continue to spin.

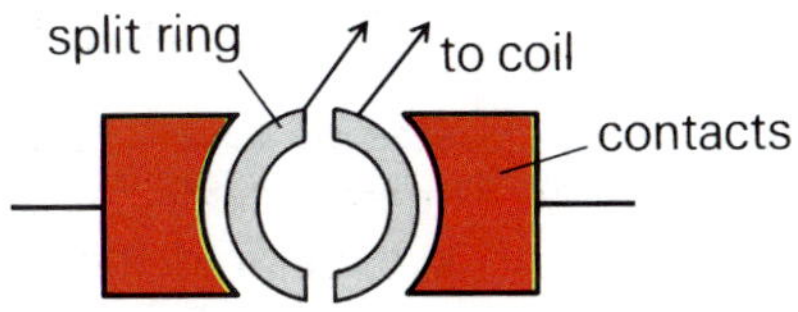

b In an old electric motor, only 70% of the electrical energy was turned into kinetic energy. Suggest two ways in which the rest of the energy may have been 'lost'.

9 Use P=I × V to calculate the working current of the electrical devices shown.

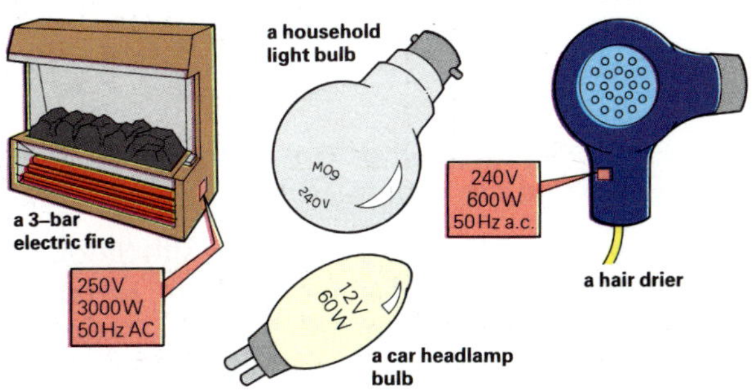

If fuses come in 2 A, 5 A and 13 A sizes, which would you use for these four devices.

10 **a** A test circuit was set up as shown, using a low resistance, 24 V power supply, an ammeter and a 1 metre length of resistance wire.

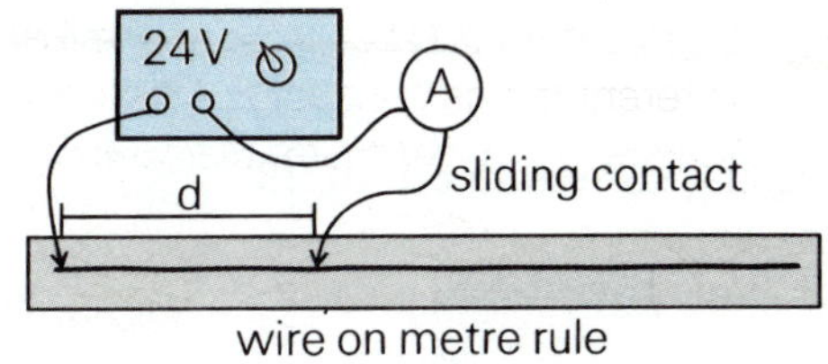

The current was measured for different lengths of wire. The results were:

length of wire (d)	33 cm	50 cm	1 m
current	2.25 A	1.5 A	0.75 A

Plot a graph of these results. From the graph:

i what current would you expect for a 75 cm length of the same wire?

ii what current would you expect if the wire was 2 m long?

b Use the formula V = I × R to calculate the resistance of the 1 m length of wire.

c Find the 'missing values' in the following table of resistors:

	R1	R2	R3	R4	R5
voltage (Volts)	?	42	63	112	?
current (Amps)	0.5	3	?	?	0.01
resistance (Ohms)	200	?	21	1120	1000

11 Describe step-by-step how electricity is generated in a coal-fired power station, transmitted across the National Grid, and used to light your classroom. Explain the energy changes and processes involved, indicating where useful energy is lost from the system and what steps are taken to minimise this loss.

Index

Photo acknowledgements

The references indicate page numbers and, where appropriate, the photo sequence.

contents page and cover: SPL. *p.3* Ander McIntyre. *p.5* top: A McIntyre/Sarah Warbrick; bottom: A McIntyre. *p.7* and *p.11* A McIntyre. *p.15* Oxfordshire Fire Services. *p.14* A McIntyre; È SPL. *p.18* A McIntyre. *p.21* David Amy. *p.25* McIntyre. *p.27* SPL. 28 *p.16* Southern Electric Photographic Unit.

The authors and publishers would like to acknowledge the kind assistance given by:

Rawley House, Oxford; Inshape Health Studios; University of Oxford Engineering Dept; Metal Salvage Ltd; Oxfordshire Fire Services; Southern Electric; Blackwell Publishers; Kidlington Airport (apron crew and welding shop); particular thanks to Jessica Ormerod.